D1150242

First published 2002
Researched and written by Martin Andrew

Produced by AA Publishing
© Automobile Association Developments Limited 2002
Illustrations © Automobile Association Developments Limited 2002
Reprinted 2004 (twice). Reprinted 2005.

Published by AA Publishing (a trading name of Automobile Association
Developments Limited, whose registered office is Southwood East, Apollo Rise,
Farnborough, Hampshire GU14 0JW;
registered number 1878835).

ISBN-10: 0 7495 3337 4
ISBN-13: 978 0 7495 3337 3

A CIP catalogue record for this book is available
from the British Library.

The contents of this book are believed correct at the time of printing.
Nevertheless, the publishers cannot be held responsible for any errors or
omissions or for changes in the details given in this book or for the
consequences of any reliance on the information it provides. This does not
affect your statutory rights. We have tried to ensure accuracy in this book, but
things do change and we would be grateful if readers would advise us of any
inaccuracies they may encounter.

We have taken all reasonable steps to ensure that these walks are
safe and achievable by walkers with a realistic level of fitness.
However, all outdoor activities involve a degree of risk and the publishers
accept no responsibility for any injuries caused to
readers whilst following these walks. For more advice on walking safely see
page 128. The mileage range shown on the front cover is
for guidance only – some walks may exceed or be less than these distances.

Visit the AA Publishing website at www.theAA.com/bookshop

Paste-up and editorial by Outcrop Publishing Services Ltd, Cumbria
for AA Publishing

A02590

Printed in Italy by G Canale & C SPA, Torino, Italy

Legend

←------	Walk route	P	Car park
••••••	Optional walk route	~~~	Cliff
-------	Adjoining footpath		Rock outcrop
—·—·—	County boundary		Beach
☀	Viewpoint	♠	Woodland
▲ 392	Spot height		Parkland
●	Built-up area	†	Church, cathedral, chapel
●	Place of interest	WC	Toilet
△	Steep section	⊼	Picnic area

Hertfordshire locator map

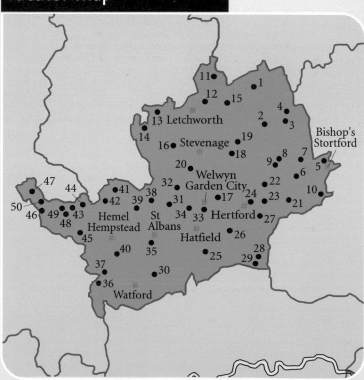

Contents

Contents

Rating: Each walk is rated for its relative difficulty compared to the other walks in this book. Walks marked 🚶🚶 🚶 🚶 are likely to be shorter and easier with little total ascent. The hardest walks are marked 🚶🚶 🚶🚶 🚶🚶 .

Walking in Safety: For advice and safety tips ➤ 128.

Introducing Hertfordshire

I could not disagree more with E M Forster's view in *Howard's End* that 'Hertfordshire is England at its quietest, with little emphasis of river and hill'. One of England's smallest counties, at a mere 630 square miles (1,632 sq km), it packs in a tremendous variety of scenery. While you will find no mountains in a county that sits like a jaunty hat above London, the chalk hills in the west and north and the boulder clay landscape of the east and centre are deeply cut by many rivers and streams. Some of these rivers have curious names that reek of ancient Britain: Mimram, Gade, Ver and Stort – short names for short rivers that merge with the Lea or Colne heading for London. Through the chalk they sparkle and dash amid lush water-meadows, the valley sides climbing up rounded bluffs to plateaux and wooded hills. Dry valleys, many of great beauty, abound in the chalk.

A glance at a map of Hertfordshire shows the Chiltern Hills to be more wooded west of Luton, with a highest point in the county at Hastoe (► Walk 46) at 800ft (244m). While the chalk hills east of Luton are not as high, the views from them north over Bedfordshire are spectacular. Upon this landscape a tapestry of roads, villages and small towns was laid during Hertfordshire's long history. Still an agricultural county, despite the commuters, the rich country of the boulder clays fed the once vast malting industry. Roads and travel were also important and most small towns have former coaching inns. The less agriculturally valuable areas were immensely popular with the wealthy and powerful, who set country mansions in their hunting grounds, and later in landscaped parks.

Sadly, several of the great medieval and Tudor palaces – Cassiobury and Theobalds to name but two – have been demolished, but a number of the great mansions, such as Hatfield House, do survive. Smaller country houses abound in their superb parks and many are encountered on these walks, such as Brocket Park, North Mymms, Knebworth, Kingswalden Bury and Rothamsted.

Before these developments, Romans came and conquered. Amazingly, their roads are still the basis of most of Hertfordshire's road system. Ermine Street, Stane Street, Watling Street and many other routes still have the power to intrigue and astonish. On many of the walks you follow or cross these roads that were first constructed nearly 2,000 years ago.

Then the Middle Ages made its impact with a rash of new towns such as Baldock in 1147 (its name, bizarrely, a corruption of Baghdad) and Royston by 1189. Others grew

---

PUBLIC TRANSPORT ⓘ

Hertfordshire is well served by public transport between the towns and major suburban villages, but considerably less so in the rural areas of such a car-orientated county. Several railway lines pass through Hertfordshire, many of them with frequent commuter stations. For transport information the County Council's web site provides excellent links to transport companies and timetables: www.hertsdirect.org.

rapidly around their castles, such as Berkhamsted, Bishop's Stortford and Hertford, whilst every village acquired its parish church.

Hertford has been the county town since Anglo-Saxon times and had certainly attained this status by 1011, when Hertfordshire is first named in records. On foot you can savour the many timber-framed and Georgian houses, here and in other towns around the county. You'll also see canals and railways of the industrial age and enjoy the spacious Garden City of Letchworth.

It is this rich history that makes this small and intricate county so fascinating. There is genuinely fine walking to be found in the gently rolling hills, along winding, deep-hedged lanes, glimpsing distinctive medieval church steeples with slender 'Hertfordshire spike' spires in the distance above the trees.

These walks are only a representative selection: another 50 could easily be suggested, and this extraordinarily richly rewarding county would still not have yielded up anywhere near all of its secrets.

Using this Book

Information panels

An information panel for each walk shows its relative difficulty (➤ 5), the distance and total amount of ascent. An indication of the gradients you will encounter is shown by the rating ▲▲▲ (no steep slopes) to ▲▲▲ (several very steep slopes).

Maps

There are 30 maps, covering 40 of the walks. Some walks have a suggested option in the same area. The information panel for these walks will tell you how much extra walking is involved. On short-cut suggestions the panel will tell you the total distance if you set out from the start of the main walk. Where an option returns to the same point on the main walk, just the distance of the loop is given. Where an option leaves the main walk at one point and returns to it at another, then the distance shown is for the whole walk. The minimum time suggested is for reasonably fit walkers and doesn't allow for stops. Each walk has a suggested map. Laminated aqua3 maps are longer lasting and water resistant.

Start Points

The start of each walk is given as a six-figure grid reference prefixed by two letters indicating which 100km square of the National Grid it refers to. You'll find more information on grid references on most Ordnance Survey maps.

Dogs

We have tried to give dog owners useful advice about how dog friendly each walk is. Please respect other countryside users. Keep your dog under control, especially around livestock, and obey local bylaws and other dog control notices.

Car Parking

Many of the car parks suggested are public, but occasionally you may find you have to park on the roadside or in a lay-by. Please be considerate when you leave your car, ensuring that access roads or gates are not blocked and that other vehicles can pass safely.

Fair on the Dewy Downs Near Therfield

A walk between Therfield and Kelshall along winding green lanes.

•DISTANCE•	3½ miles (5.7km)
•MINIMUM TIME•	1hr 30min
•ASCENT / GRADIENT•	120ft (36m) ▲▲ ▲▲
•LEVEL OF DIFFICULTY•	🚶 🚶 🚶
•PATHS•	Green lanes, tracks, field paths, village lanes, 1 stile
•LANDSCAPE•	Gently rolling arable country on chalk plateau
•SUGGESTED MAP•	aqua3 OS Explorer 194 Hertford & Bishop's Stortford
•START / FINISH•	Grid reference: TL 335370
•DOG FRIENDLINESS•	Mostly off leads but horse paddocks near Kelshall
•PARKING•	Around Therfield village green
•PUBLIC TOILETS•	None on route

BACKGROUND TO THE WALK

In the chalk hills of north east Hertfordshire you are walking in the 'champion' country – that is how it was described by contemporaries such as the early Hertfordshire historian Sir Henry Chauncey, writing in the late 17th century. The word, a corruption of the French 'champagne' or country (not the sparkling wine), describes classic, Midland, open-field farming country. Here fields were farmed in common, with holdings divided up into strips within great open fields, usually two, three or four surrounding a village. Every farmer, from the peasant to the yeoman farmer and up to the great landowner, had a share of the best and worst land. In addition there were areas of common grazing, wood and hay meadows.

Enclosure Acts
This system had immense benefits for the small farmer, but none for the more progressive and larger farmers who, over the centuries, tried to enclose the open fields for more efficient, centralised farming. This area of Hertfordshire held out longest. Kelshall's open fields were enclosed, following a private Act of Parliament, in 1795; Therfield's became enclosed as late as 1849. You can see the effects of efficiency now – vast arable fields with very, very few hedges descend northwards from the villages on the ridge to the ancient Icknield Way at the foot of the chalk downs, often their parish boundary. The area of this walk, though, is in the more intimate fields south of the villages, where the countryside is criss-crossed by ancient and attractively hedged, pre-enclosure, green lanes such as Kelshall Lane and Duck's Green, winding amid the smaller, arable fields.

Village Scenes
Therfield has a fine triangular village green with the Fox and Duck pub on its eastern side. The church was entirely rebuilt in 1878 due to subsidence. The rebuilding re-used many items from the previous, medieval church. These include piscinae, the stone basins which were usually close to the altar in a pre-Reformation church, some roof bosses and monuments, the best being that to Francis Turner, who died in 1677. The Old Rectory, south

east of the church, is also of great interest. It has a rendered, 15th-century wing and a circular stair turret. The rest of the building is a red brick, Georgian rebuild from 1767. To the west of the church are the earthworks of a motte and bailey castle. This was started by the Abbot of Ramsey during the civil wars of Stephen's reign, but was probably never completed, the motte (an artificial mound) being only 5ft (1.5m) high. Kelshall, the smaller village, retains its mainly 15th-century church, although it was extensively restored in 1870. Entry is through the original, medieval oak door and there are fragments of medieval glass. The lower part of the chancel screen also survives.

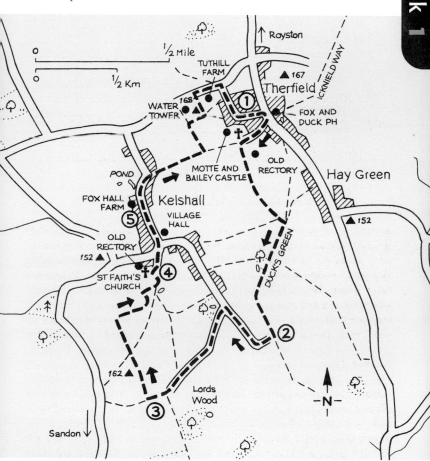

Walk 1 Directions

① From **Therfield** village green walk down **Church Lane** and into the parish churchyard. Go through a gap in the railings to the south of the south porch on to a green lane, with the vicarage garden on the left and a field on the right. At a footpath post keep straight on along a grassy margin at the left of a field, then go across a field to a kissing gate. Cross pasture to a stile and over this turn right into a green lane, **Duck's Green**. Ignoring footpaths to right and left, the track bears left, now following the parish boundary. Where the path meets a track, turn right into a green lane.

Walk 1

② Follow this green lane, which soon turns right, climbing gently between ancient hedges. At a track junction go left and continue climbing, passing a footpath junction before reaching the crest of the hill. Ignore a track turning left – carry straight on along a loosely metalled track.

> **ⓘ WHERE TO EAT AND DRINK**
> Therfield is now down to a single pub, but it is a good one. The **Fox and Duck** on the east side of the village green does food and doesn't seem to mind walkers. There is also a shop near by. Kelshall has neither pub nor shop.

③ At the crest turn right on to the bridleway, with a fence and paddocks to the left, arable land to your right. This becomes a track through arable land. At a bridleway post, where the hedge reappears, turn right into a green lane, soon hedged only on the left. At a post-and-railed sheep enclosure go left. Then, through a gate, turn left to another gate into a lane and cross to the church lychgate.

④ Visit the **Church of St Faith**, entering through its original, heavy, 15th-century door. Leave the churchyard from behind the chancel on to a path between a fence and walls, signposted 'Hertfordshire Way'. At the lane

> **ⓘ WHILE YOU'RE THERE**
> **Royston**, about 4 miles (6.4km) from Therfield, was laid out around 1189 by Royston Priory at the Ermine Street and Icknield Way crossroads. Five parishes meet at this point, three of them in Cambridgeshire. Royston has a classic long market place, now heavily encroached upon, leaving only narrow streets on each side – High Street and King Street.

> **ⓘ WHAT TO LOOK FOR**
> Inside St Faith's Church, Kelshall, at the north west angle of the north aisle, is a tall, narrow recess about 12ft (3.7m) high by 20ins (80cm) wide with a concave back and evidence that it once had a door. This unusual feature is a **banner cupboard**, for storing the staves for the parish guild banners that where used in processions and on high days and holidays, and perhaps also parish processional crosses.

turn left. At the road junction jink right then left to walk past the telephone box and the village hall, dated 1895.

⑤ Continue past **Fox Hall farm** and a pond. Turn right at a footpath sign, just before a thatched cottage, on to a track initially between hedges, then alongside a patchy hedge. At the end of the field go through the hedge and over a footbridge. Turn sharp left to walk round two sides of a small field. At the track go left to walk past the tall water tower. At the road turn right and follow it past **Tuthill Farm** and some Victorian estate cottages. Turn right past **Bell House** into **Pedlars Lane**, which winds back to **Therfield** village green.

Buntingford's Medieval Market on Ermine Street

Visit the old parish church in the fields, Wyddial village and return past a series of manor houses.

·DISTANCE·	8 miles (12.9km)
·MINIMUM TIME·	3hrs
·ASCENT / GRADIENT·	120ft (37m)
·LEVEL OF DIFFICULTY·	
·PATHS·	Tracks, lanes, field paths, village roads, 2 stiles
·LANDSCAPE·	Rolling arable countryside and Buntingford's townscape
·SUGGESTED MAP·	aqua3 OS Explorer 194 Hertford & Bishop's Stortford
·START / FINISH·	Grid reference: TL 360295
·DOG FRIENDLINESS·	On lead in horse paddocks and on pavements
·PARKING·	Buntingford High Street car park
·PUBLIC TOILETS·	At car park

BACKGROUND TO THE WALK

Buntingford grew up where Ermine Street crosses the River Rib, which is little more than a large stream here. It is also where the Baldock to Newport and Saffron Walden road crossed Ermine Street. Earlier attempts to establish a market town further north along Ermine Street foundered, first at Chipping in 1252 ('cheping' means 'market') and then at Buckland in 1258. There was a hamlet at Buntingford by 1158 and it obviously prospered at the crossroads. In 1360 Elizabeth de Burgh, the then lady of the manor of Pope's Hall, saw that Chipping could not compete and bowed to the inevitable, transferring her chartered market to Buntingford. The parish church remained at Layston, ½ mile (800m) to the east, but everything else leached to the market town. Buntingford market place was laid out in a stretch of the widened High Street. The Hare Street road junction was moved to the south, which meant that all through traffic had to cross the market place, and so pay market tolls.

Georgian Buntingford

The character of Buntingford is very much that of a prosperous, mainly Georgian, market town with some fine brick fronts. However, behind many of these are earlier, timber-framed 16th- and 17th-century buildings. At the south end is St Peter's Church, an unusual brick one with a Greek Cross plan built around 1615 as a chapel of ease to Layston's parish church. To its left is Bishop Ward's Hospital, a superb set of almshouses for four men and four women. Built of brick with stone dressings and a pedimented centre bay, they were founded in 1684 by Seth Ward. He was a local boy made good – an astronomer and mathematician as well as Bishop of Exeter and later Bishop of Salisbury. St Bartholomew's Church, the sole survivor of the deserted medieval village of Layston, is no longer functional and its nave is roofless. Wyddial church, on the other hand, is still in use and has several important features, including a brick north aisle and north chancel chapel, built in 1532 at the expense of George Canon. It also retains some fine Jacobean screens separating the chapel from the rest of the church.

Further on you pass other mansions, including Beauchamps, which was the moated manor house of a village now long vanished. The Beauchamp family owned it from the 13th to the 15th century but the house was rebuilt in the 1650s in timber-framing with large brick stacks. It was refronted in brick in the 1860s. In Buntingford, past the Railway pub, are former station buildings. These were at the terminus of a branch line which ran from St Margaret's, south of Ware, and which opened in 1863.

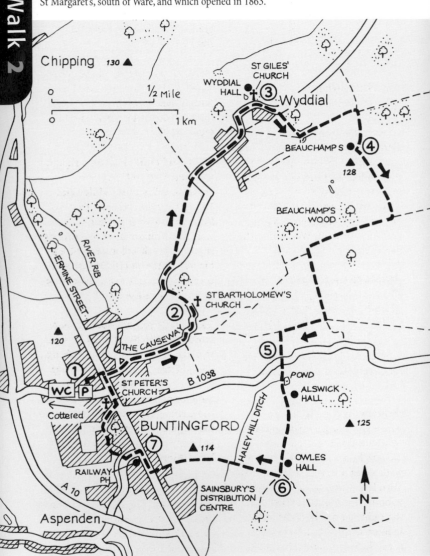

Walk 2 Directions

① From the High Street car park cross the road and turn into **Church Street**. Descend past the

Fox and Duck pub. Go left into **Wyddial Road**, then right across the River Rib ford into **The Causeway**. The lane leaves the town and becomes a winding rural lane. At a public bridleway sign turn left to

Walk 2

WHILE YOU'RE THERE

Some 3 miles (4.8km) west of Buntingford the Baldock Road passes through the delightful village of **Cottered**. It has neat, whitewashed cottages, some thatched, set well back from the large, elongated, triangular green. There is a fine church at the west end. Near by is The Lordship, a 15th-century, moated manor house.

visit what remains of St Bartholomew's Church.

② From the churchyard continue along the green lane downhill to the road. Turn right and follow the road uphill. At a bend go left at the bridleway sign, the path being a grassy baulk between arable fields. On reaching a road go straight on and wind through **Wyddial** to the parish church.

WHERE TO EAT AND DRINK

The only pubs are in Buntingford: the **Black Bull** and the **Chequers** in High Street, the **Crown** on Market Hill to the south and, in Church Road, the **Fox and Duck**. At the Aspenden Road junction is the **Railway**. Built in 1865, it is a reminder of the former railway line.

③ From the churchyard (from where you can see Wyddial Hall) continue along the road to a bend. Turn right, by a footpath sign, to walk along the right side of a hedge. Turn left at the end of the field, over a footbridge. Continue east, first on the right-hand side of the hedge, then on the left, to a farm access road. Turn right along this and walk to **Beauchamps**.

④ The route passes to the left of Beauchamps, initially alongside a neat hedge, then bears left off the concrete track on to a grassy track, with poplars on the right. Continue

to a track at the brow of the hill and turn right. Past **Beauchamp's Wood** the track gradually descends to the valley floor before turning left and gently ascending to the next crest. Turn right beside a concrete hardstanding. Descending gradually, follow the metalled track to the left.

⑤ At a road cross on to the drive to **Alswick Hall**. Passing a pond and farm buildings, then the hall itself, the route follows a green lane to **Owles Hall**.

⑥ Beyond Owles Hall turn right on to a lane. Descend westwards, to cross the valley of the **Haley Hill Ditch**. Next, ascend towards Buntingford, with the large warehouse buildings of Sainsbury's supermarket distribution centre to the left. At the end of **Owles Lane** turn right to walk along the course of Roman **Ermine Street**.

⑦ Turn left past the **Railway** pub into **Aspenden Road**, then go right into **Luynes Rise**. At a footpath sign go right, the tarmac path winding along beside the **River Rib**, with modern housing on the left. Beyond some cottages the path emerges into the **High Street**. Turn left, passing St Peter's Church and the **Seth Ward Almshouses**, to the start.

WHAT TO LOOK FOR

Wyddial Hall was built in brick in about 1516, but what you see today is mostly from 1733 and the early 19th century – stucco fronted with timber, sliding-sash windows – a bad fire precipitated these alterations. Wyddial Hall is separated from St Giles' churchyard by a brick boundary wall. It was probably built in 1532 when the north aisle and north chapel were built for George Canon (although the gateway was built later).

Hormeads Rich with Corn

A walk around Great and Little Hormead, east of the young River Quin.

•DISTANCE•	4 miles (6.4km)
•MINIMUM TIME•	2hrs
•ASCENT / GRADIENT•	85ft (26m)
•LEVEL OF DIFFICULTY•	
•PATHS•	Field paths, tracks, quiet country lanes, village road, 5 stiles
•LANDSCAPE•	Rolling arable countryside with extensive views
•SUGGESTED MAP•	aqua3 OS Explorer 194 Hertford & Bishop's Stortford
•START / FINISH•	Grid reference: TL 402298
•DOG FRIENDLINESS•	On leads on roads and in paddocks; some tricky stiles
•PARKING•	Horseshoe Hill, Great Hormead
•PUBLIC TOILETS•	None on route

BACKGROUND TO THE WALK

The Hormeads are a most attractive pair of villages in north east Hertfordshire's rich boulder-clay corn country, though Little Hormead is now merely a few houses. Indeed, much of this walk is through arable land, cut into by numerous streams heading southward towards the River Rib, with pasture around the villages.

Until 1886 the Hormeads were two separate parishes, Little to the south and Great to the north. The history of the parishes is one of steady drift northwards to Hormead Road, the east–west road which runs from Buntingford to Newport and Saffron Walden in Essex. The churches are well to the south, close to their manor houses, while 16th- and 17th-century houses are congregated along the through route, now the B1038. Along this picturesque main street, with a stream flowing along its south side, you'll see good, timber-framed houses. Some of these, such as Carter's Field and Raffles, are thatched. Turning left, past the Three Tuns pub and up Horseshoe Hill, there are more fine cottages.

To the north east of the village, up Hall Lane, is Hormead Hall. It stands in the remains of its moat, best seen as you leave the village alongside the Black Ditch stream. This timber-framed and rendered house, with its octagonal brick chimneys, was built in about 1600. Great Hormead Bury is the larger village's manor house. Its location was, however, south of the village centre, along Horseshoe Lane. St Nicholas' Church, no doubt built here for the convenience of the lord of the manor, dates initially from some time in the 13th century but is mostly 14th and 15th century in appearance. It was heavily restored in 1874, when the chancel was entirely rebuilt. A number of grotesque corbels survive, particularly in the south aisle, and, as always, give an insight into the sense of humour of medieval stone-carvers – they are mostly pulling faces at onlookers.

St Mary's, in Little Hormead, is the original church for the old parish which divided when the grander St Nicholas' Church was built. It's a more humble affair, with a Norman nave and a chancel rebuilt around 1220. The most well-known part of the church is the former north door on display inside. This has elaborate interlacing strapwork in two panels and a scrolly frieze border. The ironwork is 12th century, contemporary with fitting out the new church, and a rare survivor. The royal arms over the chancel arch is dated 1660, the year of the Restoration of Charles II, demonstrating either Royalist fervour or diplomatic nous.

131 ▲

High Hall

WOODSIDE COTTAGE

120 ▲

ANSTEY CASTLE

ST GEORGE'S CHURCH

CHEQUERS PH

Ⓑ

Ⓒ

Anstey

Meesden

SNOW END

Lincoln Hill

½ Mile

1 Km

-N-

ANSTEY BURY FARM

HERTFORDSHIRE WAY

▲ 135

Ⓓ

Ⓐ

4

THE BRICK HOUSE

HORMEAD HALL

5

BLACK DITCH

▲ 134

B 1038

Brent Pelham

River Quin

B 1368

HALL LANE

THREE TUNS PH

1

3

Great Hormead

B 1038

GT HORMEAD BURY

▲ 120

Great Hormead Park

LITTLE HORMEAD BURY FARM

2

ST MARY'S CHURCH

Little Hormead

Little Hormead Brook

BULLS FARM

Walk 3

Walk 3 Directions

① Start on **Horseshoe Hill**, a turning just west of the **Three Tuns** pub. Uphill, you bear right at the war memorial, and follow the lane to St Nicholas', the parish church of Great Hormead. From the churchyard continue along the lane, turning left at a junction that is signposted to Little Hormead and Furneux Pelham. Eventually passing **Little Hormead Bury Farm**, its barns now converted to houses, you reach the Norman parish church of Little Hormead.

WHAT TO LOOK FOR ⓘ

Although there are few good **memorials** in St Nicholas' Church in Great Hormead, one relatively modern one, near the lectern by the chancel arch, is beautifully done. It is a tender and delicate marble medallion with a bas-relief portrait of Betty who died in 1916. She was the wife of Sir Robert Romer, Lord Justice of Appeal, who lived at The Bury near by.

---

② Continue along the lane. Opposite **Bulls Farm** go left at the footpath sign into cultivated land, initially following hedges north through two fields, then turn left and right alongside a hedge to a junction. Carry straight on along a track. At first a bridleway, this becomes a footpath, leading to the main street of Great Hormead.

③ Turn right on to the road. Go beyond a left turn, **Hall Lane**. When opposite a thatched barn go to the

---

WHERE TO EAT AND DRINK ⓘ

The **Three Tuns** at the corner of Hormead Road and Horseshoe Hill serves food as well as drink. If you take the Walk 4 extension, the **Chequers** in Anstey is also welcoming.

---

left of the chevron-style bend sign to the inconspicuous start of a footpath. This follows the course of the **Black Ditch** stream, sometimes on the left side, sometimes on the right, the stream and hedge eventually bearing left. Cross the stream on a bridge into pasture and head for a footpath post at a lane. (This is Point Ⓐ, where Walk 4 turns right.)

④ Turn left to walk along the lane, initially with a hedge on the left only, then on both sides. (Walk 4 rejoins the route at Point Ⓓ from the right, at a 'Hertfordshire Way' footpath sign.) The lane continues winding gently downhill – you will see an electricity pylon on the left. Pass beneath its cables to go left at a footpath sign on to a track, with a hedge to your right. Over the brow descend towards **Hormead Hall**. Go to the right of a cattle grid to a stile, then head diagonally left across pasture to another stile.

WHILE YOU'RE THERE

About 3 miles (4.8km) east of Anstey is the picturesque, remote and small **Church of St Mary's**, Meesden, reached along a track. The church has a Norman nave but its best feature is a remarkable porch from about 1530 with the archway, east window, corbel table and battlements, all in moulded Tudor brick.

---

⑤ Once over this go left along the edge of an arable field. Look to the left here, through the hedge, to see the remains of Hormead Hall's medieval moat. Turn left out of the field on to a lane and then turn right along another, **Hall Lane**, to a road junction. Turn right into **Hormead Road**, the main street of Great Hormead. A left turn past the **Three Tuns** pub returns you to **Horseshoe Hill**.

The Mermen's Tale

Extend the walk with a circuit past a rare, brick house to Anstey.
See map and information panel for Walk 3

•DISTANCE•	8 miles (12.9km)
•MINIMUM TIME•	3hrs 30min
•ASCENT / GRADIENT•	75ft (23m)
•LEVEL OF DIFFICULTY•	

Walk 4 Directions (Walk 3 option)

From Point Ⓐ turn right to walk past **The Brick House** with its crow-step gables. Built in the 1570s for Thomas Brand, a yeoman farmer, it shows a very early use of brick at this social level in 16th-century Hertfordshire – the name underlines its rarity.

Continue to some farm buildings. Turn left before the last one, then go left and right along a track beside a stream, with a hedge reappearing at the parish boundary. At a lane turn left to **Anstey Bury Farm**, crossing the road junction to a footpath sign. Across a paddock, head straight over arable land to a bridge, then again to another bridge. Now on a grass track, ascend to an electricity pole. Turn left and, where the track goes left, continue straight on, across a footbridge to Anstey, Point Ⓑ.

Follow a winding lane signposted 'Nuthampstead and Barkway'. When you reach a footpath sign turn left, through the garden, to **Woodside Cottage**. Pass some woods and continue straight on to a concrete road (Point Ⓒ) – this skirts to the

right of Anstey Castle's motte and bailey. There was once a stone keep on the 35ft (11m) high motte and the castle was held by the great Geoffrey de Mandeville, Sheriff of Hertfordshire in the 12th century, who also held South Mimms Castle.

Continue to the memorable **St George's Church**. It has a late Norman central crossing and a chancel dating from about 1300, medieval graffiti and 14th-century misericord seats. The highlight, perhaps, is the late Norman font with a frieze of four mermen holding their fish tails.

Leave the churchyard via the lychgate. Turn right along the main road, descending to cross the stream, then out of the valley to **Snow End**. Carry straight on, signposted 'Brent Pelham'. At the sign to Silver Street, bear right on to a track. At the end turn left on to a footpath, then turn right alongside a ditch and vestigial hedge, the **Hertfordshire Way**. Follow this across a valley to a crest. Here it bears right to a footbridge, and left through the parish boundary hedge between Anstey and Hormead. Go straight across cultivated land, towards a footpath signpost beside a copse, Point Ⓓ. Turn right, on to the lane, to rejoin Walk 3.

Under the Bishop's Eye

A walk from Bishop's Stortford's historic town centre.

•DISTANCE•	5 miles (8km)
•MINIMUM TIME•	2hrs 15min
•ASCENT / GRADIENT•	165ft (50m)
•LEVEL OF DIFFICULTY•	
•PATHS•	Pavement, tracks, green lanes and field paths, 5 stiles
•LANDSCAPE•	Historic townscape and woodland on low ridge
•SUGGESTED MAP•	aqua3 OS Explorer 194 Hertford & Bishop's Stortford
•START / FINISH•	Grid reference: TL 488215
•DOG FRIENDLINESS•	On leads on pavements and around Wickham Hall
•PARKING•	Causeway car park, off Old River Lane
•PUBLIC TOILETS•	At foot of Waytemore Castle motte and Jackson Square shopping centre, south of Bridge Street

Walk 5 Directions

From the car park turn right up **Bridge Street**. Its timber-framed buildings make Bridge Street one of the best surviving streets in the town. Go straight on, past the 1828 Corn Exchange, into **High Street**, to visit **St Michael's Church**. This remarkably complete, early 15th-century church has retained its north and south porch doors, chancel screen and choir stalls with interesting misericord carvings. The tower was heightened in brick and the lead spire was added in 1812.

Out of the church turn left into **Windhill**. At the roundabout go right into **Bells Hill** and shortly go left on to the **Hertfordshire Way**. This descends to the grounds of **Bishop's Stortford College**, joining a tarmac path for a while. At the crest turn right, still on the Hertfordshire Way, alongside a hedge. Once through a gate go left along **Maze Green Road**. Go left to another gate, the footpath signed

'Cradle End', to turn right, with playing fields on the left. The path continues through scrubby woodland, turning right along garden fences and round the corner. With houses soon on both sides, cross an estate road up **Squire's Close**. The path continues across another estate road and, beyond the houses, crosses the **A1184**.

> ### WHERE TO EAT AND DRINK
> Bishop's Stortford has pubs all over the town. **Scruffy Mac's** on the corner of Devoils Lane, is a distasteful renaming of the mostly 16th-century, timber-framed Black Lion. The **George Hotel** is at the corner of High Street and North Street. There are also restaurants and cafés in Jackson Square shopping centre.

Once over the stile walk alongside a hedge, still on the Hertfordshire Way. Descend alongside woods to go through a hedge and turn right on to a green lane. Passing under the **A120**, the Roman Stane Street, the Hertfordshire Way turns left but you go straight on, along an access road signed 'Hadham Lodge'. Once

WHAT TO LOOK FOR ⓘ

St Michael's Church, Bishop's Stortford, is a grand town church rebuilt in the early 15th century. The choir stalls are reputedly from the old St Paul's in London. Their misericords, or tip-up seats, have carvings underneath, including angel and human heads, an owl, dragon, swan and other animals.

past a pond and to the left of Hadham Lodge, walk alongside a paddock fence. When it ends go straight on. The lane beyond the woods becomes a grassy track with **Bloodhounds Wood** to the left. Cross a junction and continue on to the crest. Here the path bears right on to a hedgeless track, briefly within Essex. Continue past the beech trees in the grounds of **Wickham Hall** to your right. You get a reasonable view of Wickham Hall, with its large chimneystacks. It consists of two separate Tudor houses, joined together in the late 17th century to form a single, L-plan house.

At the corner turn left past a bungalow and then right by a mast. The track winds along the county boundary. Where the fence ends, turn sharp right descending to walk along the edge of some trees. At the footpath sign go left over a stile into pasture and head alongside the hedge to the bypass bridge. Just through the bridge ignore a gate ahead and go through the one on the right, with a footpath sign. The path follows the edge of some woods, briefly entering them and later continuing alongside.

Cross the road to a stile. Descend diagonally to the field's lowest point in the far corner. Cross a stream and head for a big oak by the hedge, with a stile beyond it. Cross a green

lane through the hedge-and-tree belt. Now skirt a cricket pitch to the diagonally opposite corner and leave the field on a path with allotments to your right. Cross to **Elm Road** and at the petrol station turn right into **Northgate End**.

Bishop's Stortford grew up at a strategic ford on the **River Stort**. Here Roman Stane Street crossed the water on its route east from its Ermine Street junction, near Puckeridge, to Colchester. The original ford was abandoned and the medieval town migrated about 600yds (549m) south to another ford, this time guarded by the Bishop of London's great castle.

At the roundabout turn left past **Northgate End car park**, bearing left on to a path and passing through **Link Road car park** to the gate near the bridge.

Waytemore Castle was built on the east bank of the river opposite the town, soon after the Norman Conquest of 1066. Traffic diverted south through the market had tolls collected before crossing the ford or, later, a medieval bridge. The crossing was in the lee of the castle, whose 40ft (12.2m) motte is crowned by the remains of a stone shell keep. At the motte of Waytemore Castle cross **Link Road** back to the **Causeway car park**.

WHILE YOU'RE THERE ⓘ

Bishop's Stortford has two very different museums. The **Rhodes Memorial and Commonwealth Centre** in South Road is the house where Cecil Rhodes, the African coloniser and founder of Rhodesia (now Zimbabwe), was born in 1853. The **Local History Museum** is in the former cemetery foreman's house on Jervis Road.

Gorgeous Palace, Solemn Temple

A walk through Much Hadham, one of Hertfordshire's best villages.

•DISTANCE•	4½ miles (7.2km)
•MINIMUM TIME•	2hrs 30min
•ASCENT / GRADIENT•	115ft (35m) ▲ ▲ ▲
•LEVEL OF DIFFICULTY•	🚶 🚶 🚶
•PATHS•	Field paths and tracks, 4 stiles
•LANDSCAPE•	Gentle hills and steep river bank
•SUGGESTED MAP•	aqua3 OS Explorer 194 Hertford & Bishop's Stortford
•START / FINISH•	Grid reference: TL 428197
•DOG FRIENDLINESS•	Off lead except in pastures and around Moor Place
•PARKING•	North end of High Street, just south of B1004 left turn
•PUBLIC TOILETS•	None on route

BACKGROUND TO THE WALK

Much Hadham, nestling in the valley of the River Ash, was on a minor route from Bishop's Stortford to Ware, but owes its architectural quality to the Bishop of London. His stronghold, Waytemore Castle, was at Bishop's Stortford 5 miles (8km) away and Much Hadham had been given to the Bishopric in the will of Queen Ethefleda in AD 991. Before 1066 one Bishop of London had built a residence here, but the Bishop's Palace, seen from within the churchyard, was rebuilt in the early 16th century on a letter-H plan. It was refaced in brick at the end of the 17th century and has been altered since. By 1817 it had become a private lunatic asylum, and it was converted into a private house in 1888.

Hertfordshire Spike

The mostly 13th- to 15th-century church is quite large due to the patronage of the bishops. The tower is known to have been built by Bishop Robert de Braybrooke (Bishop of London, 1381–1401). It is crowned by a tall 'Hertfordshire spike' lead-clad spire. The king and queen's head label stops to the tower west door are 20th century, by Henry Moore. The Palace and parish church stand to the east of the High Street. This is one of the best village streets in the county and fully the equal of those over the border in Essex. The architecture is a mixture of 16th- and 17th-century timber-framed houses. Many of these are 'jettied' (their upper storeys are projecting) and plastered, and present Georgian brick, indicating either refronted timber-framed houses or newly built ones. There is also a sprinkling of Victorian activity, such as the yellow brickwork on the 'new' Manor House of 1839.

North of the Palace, The Lordship is a grand, Georgian house from about 1745 with a Tudor rear wing and a large Georgian stable block, all screened by iron railings and gates. Back past Church Lane the variety of buildings is wonderful and there are stretches of picturesque pebbled pavement. Look especially for the former Ye Olde Red Lion Hotel. Jettied and timber-framed, it was built in the 16th century as an inn. The Hall, set back from the road, was constructed in 1735 and the Bull Inn has been a tavern since 1727 (or possibly earlier). Castle House is 17th-century but has a pretty, 'Gothicky' refronting and the Forge

Museum was a blacksmith's shop in 1811. You leave the village at the war memorial by Harry Wilson, a leading Art and Crafts architect and sculptor. West of the village is Moor Place, a country house set in parkland and built between 1777 and 1779. It was constructed for James Garden by Robert Mitchell. Much Hadham also played a small role in the history of the monarchy. Edmund Tudor, the father of the future Henry VII, was born in the Bishop's Palace in about 1430.

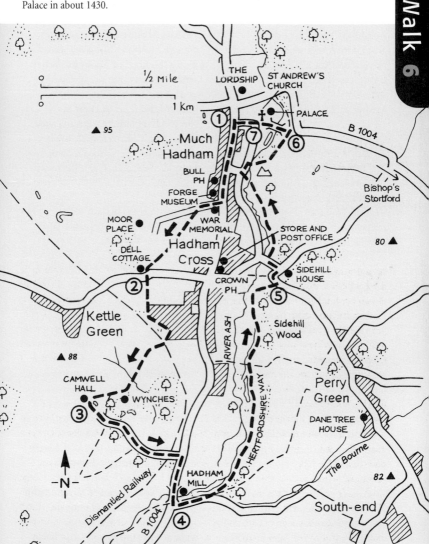

Walk 6 Directions

① Walk along the **High Street** into the village, going right just before the war memorial, over a stile beside ball-finialled gate piers. Follow the drive, then go left to a stile at the corner of some tennis courts. Now in the parkland to **Moor Place**, head diagonally to skirt to the left of some farm

Walk 6

WHERE TO EAT AND DRINK ⓘ
Directly on the route is the **Bull**, serving good food. Down the High Street past the war memorial but before the Kettle Green Road junction is the **Crown**.

buildings. Then go to the right-hand corner of a wood and join a farm access track. Cross the drive on to a metalled track, then bear left along a granite slabway to a kissing gate beside **Dell Cottage**.

② Cross over the road to a footpath signed 'Windmill Way' and cross an arable field, heading to the left of a rendered cottage. Follow a track behind gardens to the road which bears right past a telephone box, becoming a metalled lane and later a hedgeless track amid cultivated land. Where this swings left, carry straight on to the valley floor, bearing right at some cottages, still along the field edge. Head towards **Camwell Hall**, an attractive 15th-century hall house.

③ At the farm bear left on to its access drive, which becomes a lane, passing **Wynches**, an early 19th-century stucco villa on the left. Turn right on to the **B1004** to descend to **Hadham Mill**. Turn left at the lane after crossing the bridge over the **River Ash**.

④ Follow the lane and go left through a gate with a bridleway and Hertfordshire Way signs. Turn right along the track and then bear left, not uphill to the right. Follow this

delightful, well-waymarked path, with steeply sloping woods to your right and the river to your left. Eventually you will come to a lane.

⑤ Go left here and follow it to turn left at a T-junction by **Sidehill House**. At a kissing gate go right, signed 'Hertfordshire Way', to walk along the floor of a pastoral valley with the River Ash meandering to your left. On reaching a lane go straight on, then go right at the 'Public Footpath 21' sign over the River Ash. Climb steeply through a copse. Turn left on to a metalled lane, the wooded river cliff now to your left.

WHILE YOU'RE THERE ⓘ
Henry Moore lived at **Dane Tree House** in Perry Green, a mile (1.6km) south east of Much Hadham. He moved here in 1941, after his London studio had been bombed, and remained until his death in 1986. The house is owned by the Henry Moore Foundation. Conducted tours are possible on some summer afternoons, by written appointment.

⑥ Just before the road junction go left at a public footpath sign. Bear left (not straight on) to descend steeply on a holloway track through the woods down to the river. Cross the footbridge and follow the path to the churchyard.

⑦ Visit **St Andrew's Church**. From the churchyard you can get an excellent view of the Bishop's Palace. Continue westwards, back to the **High Street**.

WHAT TO LOOK FOR
On the west side of the High Street is the **Forge Museum**, a blacksmith's shop and cottage donated to the Hertfordshire Building Preservation Trust in 1988 by Jean Page, daughter of the last blacksmith. He had died in 1983, the great grandson of Frederick Page who started the business in 1811. Open from 11AM to 5PM on Fridays, Saturdays, Sundays and Bank Holiday Mondays, it again has a working smithy.

When Queen Elizabeth Slept in Hadham Hall

A circuit of the picturesque 'ends' and hamlets of Little Hadham and out to Hadham Hall.

•DISTANCE•	4 miles (6.4km)
•MINIMUM TIME•	1hr 45min
•ASCENT / GRADIENT•	125ft (100m)
•LEVEL OF DIFFICULTY•	
•PATHS•	Field paths, tracks, roads and village pavements, 2 stiles
•LANDSCAPE•	Gentle rolling hills and valley
•SUGGESTED MAP•	aqua3 OS Explorer 194 Hertford & Bishop's Stortford
•START / FINISH•	Grid reference: TL 440228
•DOG FRIENDLINESS•	Mostly arable country but lead needed on pavements
•PARKING•	Albury Road, Little Hadham (north of traffic lights at A120 crossroads)
•PUBLIC TOILETS•	None on route

BACKGROUND TO THE WALK

As with many villages walked through in this book, Little Hadham has moved about. It was originally focused around the parish church at Church End in a common Anglo-Saxon location, that is away from an old Roman road. It migrated westwards to a more important crossroads around 1600, leaving the medieval church and a couple of farms isolated between it and Hadham Hall. The church is about 200yds (183m) north of the Roman road, known to the Anglo-Saxons as Stane Street ('stone-paved road').

Riverside Development

It was natural that development should accumulate at the crossroads and the bridge over the young River Ash. The houses here include the late medieval Bridge End, altered in 1732, The Whare, partly from about 1500 and timber-framed with four octagonal stacks, and 17th-century Brook House. There was also the Angel inn, whose sign bracket remains on a chequer-brick, 18th-century house. St Cecilia's Church, 600yds (549m) east of the crossroads, has fittings probably given by Arthur Capell, once the lord of the manor in Hadham Hall. These include a pulpit dated 1633, which was installed following a critical report by the Bishop's visitor earlier that year.

Housing Development

A further 600yds (549m) east of the church stands Hadham Hall. The hall is the seat of the manor of Little Hadham, a cluster of 16th- and 17th-century buildings grouped around a grassed courtyard. A small estate of modern housing behind it has been named Baud Close after earlier lords of the manor. The north side of the yard has stables and cottages with fake timber-framing from around 1900. These have now also been converted into housing. The south side of the courtyard has a former gatehouse (now offices) built in brick, and possibly earlier than the hall itself.

Hadham Hall

To the east is Hadham Hall itself, part of a very large courtyard house built for Henry Capell in the 1570s and completed by 1578, when Queen Elizabeth visited him here. What you see is the west range with its central gatehouse flanked by three-storey, battlemented towers and a part of the south range. The north and east ranges and over half the south range were pulled down around 1668 when Arthur Capell, created Earl of Essex by Charles II in 1661, moved to Cassiobury, near Watford. The surviving work gives a good idea of the hall's scale and quality, for every window has a pediment and the brick frames and mullions are rendered to look like stone.

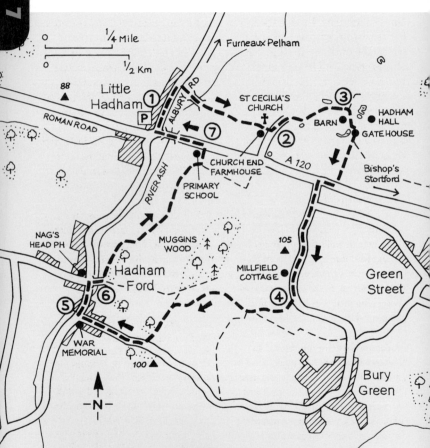

Walk 7 Directions

① Walk uphill on **Albury Road**, to a footpath sign on the right 'To Church ½ and Bishop's Stortford 2¾'. Take this path alongside an arable field, which descends to the **River Ash**, here merely a small stream. Cross the footbridge to climb on to a grassy baulk between fields. This leads to the church, whose tower peeps from its churchyard surrounded by trees.

② Leave the churchyard with the many-gabled rear of **Church End farmhouse** on your right to enter a

Walk 7

lane. Go left, past the old church hall (now converted to a bungalow). Follow the track round to the right of some farm buildings to climb to the brow of the hill. At a public bridleway junction-post turn right. The modern little development of houses called **Baud Close** stands behind a fine brick-built barn, which has also now been converted into a house.

③ From the central grassed courtyard of **Hadham Hall** and its outbuildings, pass the 1570s gatehouse to walk down the lime avenue to the main road, the A120 or Roman **Stane Street**. Turn right and shortly turn left down **Millfield Lane**. This junction is the highest point on the walk.

④ Beyond **Millfield Cottage** go right, on to a metalled green lane by a public byway sign where the lane turns left. At a fork go right, still on the hedged green lane. Passing the splendidly named **Muggins Wood**, climb to a lane, the path now overhung by trees. Turn right and follow the lane, descending into **Hadham Ford**.

⑤ At the junction, with the war memorial in a small triangular green, turn right along the main street. The lane crosses the river. At a public footpath sign opposite the **Nag's Head** pub turn to the right, across a footbridge leading to a stile.

⑥ Over the stile turn left and head for the left-hand corner of a wood, the modest river on your left. Continue uphill to the stile by a gate, joining a track which curves right, past some trees, and then goes left between arable fields with St Celia's Church in Little Hadham visible ahead. The path passes paddocks on the left, then jinks past a primary school, emerging on to the **A120** past a single-storey thatched cottage.

⑦ Turn left along the pavement, past the school, to the traffic lights. Cross the river bridge to the group of buildings at the staggered central crossroads. Turn right here, back into **Albury Road**.

Walk 8

Romans in the Rib Valley

From Standon to Braughing and back along the Rib Valley.

•DISTANCE•	5 miles (8km)
•MINIMUM TIME•	2hrs 30min
•ASCENT / GRADIENT•	190ft (57m) ▲ ▲ ▲
•LEVEL OF DIFFICULTY•	林 林 林
•PATHS•	Tracks, paths, some roads, and former railway line, 5 stiles
•LANDSCAPE•	Winding valley of River Rib
•SUGGESTED MAP•	aqua3 OS Explorer 194 Hertford & Bishop's Stortford
•START / FINISH•	Grid reference: TL 396223
•DOG FRIENDLINESS•	Mostly arable farmland
•PARKING•	High Street, Standon (off A120)
•PUBLIC TOILETS•	None on route

BACKGROUND TO THE WALK

It is difficult to visualise a prosperous Roman town in the fields between Puckeridge and Braughing on the west bank of the River Rib. The eastern boundary is roughly along the trackbed of a railway, itself also vanished into history. A look at the OS map shows the site roughly between the boundary north of Braughing Station House and south to a line between the pub symbol and the Sluice. Here Ermine Street changes its alignment. Having headed north east to Puckeridge and along its High Street to the Roman town, it deviated to head north west to Buntingford. Stane Street, from Colchester in the east via Bishop's Stortford, met Ermine Street near the pub symbol, but in medieval times the road moved south to pass through Standon from Horse Cross, possibly because the river crossing at Standon was easier. To the west of Horse Cross on the OS map the parish boundaries follow the course of Stane Street.

Other Roman roads converged here, including one that is now a track and heads south east from Baldock towards the Roman town. It disappears in Hamels Park with its landscaped grounds. Another one from Verulamium (St Albans) merged with Ermine Street 2 miles (3.2km) south of the town site. The present B1368 to Barkway and Cambridge follows the course of a Roman road due north from the Roman town. Interestingly the diversion of Stane Street south through Standon spawned a new settlement at the Ermine Street junction. This was Puckeridge, which was granted a market charter in 1311.

The walk goes through an area steeped in Roman history but there is much else besides. For example, there is the fine, wide High Street of Standon – it used to be the market place. It has two timber-framed pubs and several well-preserved houses. It also has a church at the south – its once detached 15th-century tower and 'Hertfordshire spike' spirelet rear over the Georgian houses. Inside, the Sadleir monuments of 1587 and 1606 are worth looking for. Out in the country, Upp Hall, east of Braughing, is a fine, brick mansion from about 1640 with three, widely-spaced gables. To its north stands a great brick barn, probably earlier in date. Braughing, delightfully dependent on the River Quin and its two fords, has a sound church in which the Brograve monument from 1625 is outstanding. More contemporarily, Braughing Station is now a house but it retains a platform. It was on the Buntingford branch line which opened in 1863 and closed in 1964.

Green
End

St Mary's
Church

94 ▲ **6**

5

H & N JONES

AXE AND
COMPASSES
PH

120 ▲

FORD ST

BROWN
BEAR PH

Braughing

4

RIVER QUIN

RIVER RIB

A 10

BRAUGHING
STATION HOUSE

ROMAN TOWN
(SITE OF)

7

Sacombe
Wood

BARN

UPP HALL

3

B 1368

Harcamlow Way

DISMANTLED
RAILWAY

86 ▲

100 ▲

Puckeridge

Braughing Warren Bourne

SCHOOL

Bishop's Stortford

8

Station
Road

STANDON
FLOUR MILLS

2

A 120

A 120

BELL PH

96 ▲

Standon

1

PAPER
MILL HOUSE

STAR PH

A HADHAM RD

THE
LORDSHIP

½ Mile

B

½ Km

Walk 8

Walk 8 Directions

① Walk south along **Standon High Street** to the church. At the junction with **Paper Mill Lane** (Point Ⓐ, where Walk 9 diverges) go left into **Hadham Road**. Beyond the village turn left at a public footpath signposted 'Frogshall Cottages'. Go sharp left along the edge of a cultivated field and continue as the path becomes a green lane descending to the **A120**. Turn right, uphill. Before the bend, go left at a public bridleway sign.

② Follow the green lane, which eventually descends into a valley to bear right, keeping a stream on your right. At the end of the arable field cross the parish boundary to climb away from the stream, with oak woods on your right. Pass to the right of some old farm buildings to a road.

③ Cross to a bridleway sign by the post box. Keep alongside a metal park fence to skirt **Upp Hall** house. Now cross to the corner of the field into a green lane, initially with woods away to your left, to ascend to a lane.

④ Go left on to the lane and follow this until, passing some cottages, go to the left of No 28, on to a path that passes behind gardens to your right and descends to the road.

⑤ Here, in **Braughing**, turn left, then turn right at the **Square** into St Mary's churchyard. From the church descend to the lane junction with **Church End**. Turn right down **Fleece Lane**. This becomes a footpath, which crosses the **River Quin** on an iron bridge and climbs to the main road.

⑥ Turn left briefly on to the **B1368**, then left again down **Malting Lane**. A footbridge bypasses the River Quin ford. Turn right into **Ford Street**. Once out of the village turn left on to the **B1368**, shortly crossing the **River Rib**.

> **WHERE TO EAT AND DRINK** ⓘ
> Standon has the **Bell** in the High Street and, opposite the church, the **Star**. Standon's several shops include a baker's. The next refreshment is found in Braughing at the **Axe and Compasses** and the **Brown Bear**.

⑦ Go left at a footpath sign just before an old railway bridge. Bear right to the former trackbed to turn left on to it – the Roman town site is on your right. Follow the track, sometimes beside it, with the river to the left. Eventually pass a school on your right and bear right at a signpost to cross the trackbed. At a cul-de-sac, **Meadow Walk**, turn right to **Station Road**.

⑧ Turn left along **Station Road** and left on to the main road, the **A120**. Pass the former **Standon Flour Mills** dated 1901. Cross the road at the crossing, then cross the **River Rib bridge**. Turn right and you are back in the **High Street**.

> **WHAT TO LOOK FOR** ⓘ
> After St Mary's Church in Braughing you go down **Fleece Lane** which is ceremonially swept and the funeral bell tolled every year on 2nd October in accordance with the will of Mathew Wall. The ritual commemorates his extreme good fortune -- in having two funerals. At his first, a pallbearer slipped on wet leaves in Fleece Lane. Wall's coffin fell and as it hit the ground, he woke up! Saved from the horror of being buried alive, he lived on and raised a family, dying some 30 years later in 1595.

A Mighty Subject's House

Extend Walk 8 with a circuit of water-meadows and The Lordship.
See map and information panel for Walk 8

Walk 9

•DISTANCE•	1½ miles (2.4km)
•MINIMUM TIME•	1hr
•ASCENT / GRADIENT•	Negligible
•LEVEL OF DIFFICULTY•	👫 👫 👫

Walk 9 Directions (Walk 8 option)

Point Ⓐ is a small green with an oak tree commemorating King George V's coronation in 1911. Turn right down **Paper Mill Lane**. Beyond some farm buildings on the right the lane curves left and crosses the course of an old railway.

After **Paper Mill House** and just before the **River Rib ford**, go left through a gate at a bridleway sign. Continue along the right-hand side of a wire fence, hedged in places, now in pasture and alongside the course of the old railway. Through a gate carry straight on, the railway gradually bearing left. Follow the line of electricity poles. **The Lordship** is in view, seen to the right, across the river.

According to two date stones, The Lordship was built in 1546. A third stone bears the coat of arms and initials of the builder, Sir Ralph Sadleir. He was one of the richest commoners in Tudor England and a principal Secretary of State to Henry VIII in the early 1540s. This great courtyard house was mostly demolished around 1830, leaving only the arched gateway and west wing and half of the south range, together with other fragments. In 1872 it was adapted and new ranges built, assuming much of its present, romantic, 'Tudor' form. It served as a hunting lodge for the 2nd Duke of Wellington, the son of the Prime Minister and victor of Waterloo. A new wing was added after a fire in 1925. The effect is quite delightful, with the pinnacled gables and diagonally-set clusters of chimneystacks.

Go through a gate and turn right into a bridleway between hedges. This winds and descends, with arable fields to the left, turning right to cross the river (Point Ⓑ). Go through another gate, then walk alongside a fence through pasture to a further gate.

You can enjoy more views of **The Lordship** to your right as you cross its gravelled drive to a kissing gate. The path descends towards the river bank through pasture and there is another good view of The Lordship behind you. Where the river turns right, carry straight on to a gate in the hedge ahead. Through this, turn right on to a metalled track. Re-cross the **River Rib** using the ford bypass footbridge, to follow **Paper Mill Lane** back into **Standon** and Point Ⓐ.

Sawbridgeworth: a Market Town on the Stort

From Sawbridgeworth walk along the Stort Navigation and back through Pishiobury Park.

·DISTANCE·	4 miles (6.4km)
·MINIMUM TIME·	2hrs
·ASCENT / GRADIENT·	55ft (17m)
·LEVEL OF DIFFICULTY·	
·PATHS·	Canal tow path, field and parkland paths and some streets
·LANDSCAPE·	Gentle countryside, parkland and wide, shallow valley
·SUGGESTED MAP·	aqua3 OS Explorer 194 Hertford & Bishop's Stortford
·START / FINISH·	Grid reference: TL 481148
·DOG FRIENDLINESS·	No problems but lead advisable on town stretches
·PARKING·	Bell Street car park, Sawbridgeworth
·PUBLIC TOILETS·	At Bell Street (East) car park

Walk 10 Directions

This part of Hertfordshire has always been rich barley country. In the Domesday Book of 1089 it was recorded that Sawbridgeworth was the most valuable estate in the county with two-thirds of its land under the plough.

Turn right from the car park into **Bell Street**. Sawbridgeworth is a delightful market town, despite the fact that most of its buildings lack the grandeur of nearby Bishop's Stortford. Bell Street is a good example, it's a street of well-preserved Georgian and timber-framed houses, some re-fronted.

Go straight on across the junction of the **Square** and **Knight Street** into **Church Street**. In 1222 Sawbridgeworth received its first market charter, which was renewed in 1306. Two annual fairs were granted to the Leventhorpe family

of Pishiobury in 1447 so its grid of streets is long established. The market place runs from Far Green northwards to Church Street, but later encroachment to the east of the Square has blurred the plan.

Pass the 1652 **Church House** (clad in painted weatherboarding) to enter **Great St Mary's churchyard**. The church is built mostly of flint with stone dressings but it has a striking Tudor, red brick stair turret added to its tower. Since it was an important and rich market-town church, the local gentry filled it with their memorials, including fine brasses and wall monuments. The grandest are the marble one to

---

WHERE TO EAT AND DRINK

Try the **Bell** in Bell Street and the **Market House Hotel** at the junction with Knight Street (the latter being a 16th-century, timber-framed building jettied to both streets). Out of town, where you leave the Stort Navigation, are the **Riverside Restaurant** and the **Harlow Mill**.

George, Viscount Hewyt of Gowram from 1689, and the Jacobean one to Sir John Leventhorpe and his wife from 1625. The best brass is the 1430s, life-size pair to another Sir John Leventhorpe and his wife.

Once out of the church, continue downhill to the south east corner of the churchyard and into a close of quirky, 1920s brick and flint cottages. Continue on the path, now between garden boundaries, to the road. Here turn left to leave the town. At **Sheering Mill**, **Lock Number 6** – the mill now replaced by housing – turn right on to the tow path of the Stort Navigation. The River Stort was canalised in 1769. It has 15 locks along 13 miles (20.9km) of canalised river. The collapse of Roydon lock in 1909 ended the canal's commerce, exporting malt and grain and importing ash, wood and coal. Follow the tow path for nearly 2 miles (3.2km), firstly on the Hertfordshire bank and then across a footbridge to the Essex bank. Along this pretty walk with water-meadows, dragonflies and willows, you will also get glimpses of Pishiobury Park.

You reach the road at the **Riverside Restaurant** with the **Harlow Mill** pub on the opposite corner. Turn right over the Stort bridge, then turn right again at the footpath sign between the modern flats, **Riverside Court**, and the river bank. Go over two footbridges then through a kissing gate to continue along the river bank. At a post-and-wire fence go left, away from the river, then turn right through a kissing gate to walk parallel to the left boundary of the meadows. Go left over a footbridge to a grass track alongside

a hedge, heading towards houses lining the old drive to **Pishiobury Park**. Passing between garden fences, you cross **Pishiobury Drive** – to your right is the west front of the mansion.

By 1534 Pishiobury had been 'emparked' as a hunting park. The mansion was rebuilt by Walter Mildmay around 1570. Some of this survives, although the appearance, which includes battlemented brickwork, is that of James Wyatt's rebuilding after a fire in 1782. His stucco render was removed in 1904, exposing much Tudor brickwork, while the stables and barn are still basically Tudor. The park itself was converted to 18th-century Picturesque by 'Capability' Brown.

Across the drive you join the **Pishiobury Park Circular Walk** through a kissing gate. Through another kissing gate you enter proper parkland. At the crest bear left into an avenue of oaks and horse chestnuts, the avenue veering right along the ridge. Leave the parkland through a kissing gate. Carry straight on, along a path between gardens. Cross over a road then descend to a footbridge over a stream. Climb out of the valley on to another road and go along a path diagonally right, beside the cricket club entrance. Emerging at **Far Green**, go left past the **Old Manse** to the **Square**, and left back into **Bell Street**.

WHILE YOU'RE THERE

For a complete contrast, visit **Harlow New Town**, across the Essex boundary to the south of the Stort Navigation. Instituted under the New Towns Act of 1946, it was planned by Sir Frederick Gibberd in 1947 and intended for London's overspill population.

Plague Strikes in Ashwell

See evidence of the bubonic plague before strolling along the chalky downs.

•DISTANCE•	6½ miles (10.4km)
•MINIMUM TIME•	2hrs 30min
•ASCENT / GRADIENT•	140ft (43m) ▲▲▲
•LEVEL OF DIFFICULTY•	林 林 林
•PATHS•	Tracks and paths, some lanes around Ashwell, 1 stile
•LANDSCAPE•	Arable chalk downs and muddy plain
•SUGGESTED MAP•	aqua3 OS Explorers 193 Luton & Stevenage; 208 Bedford & St Neots
•START / FINISH•	Grid reference: TL 268396 (on Explorer 193)
•DOG FRIENDLINESS•	Mostly arable land, some cattle approaching Ashwell
•PARKING•	East end of High Street, outside United Reformed church
•PUBLIC TOILETS•	Recreation Ground off Lucas Lane

BACKGROUND TO THE WALK

One of the most moving things you will see on any of these walks is the graffiti on the north wall inside the tower of St Mary's Church in Ashwell. High up the wall is a graffito inscription in Latin which translated says 'The first plague was in 1349', and lower down a more desperate one, 'Miserable, wild, distracted, the dregs of the people alone survive to witness, 1350' while the last in the series refers to a great storm, 'At the end of the second (plague) a tempest full mighty this year 1361 St Maur thunders in the heavens'.

Black Death

The graffiti bear a remarkable witness to the Black Death, the bubonic plague spread by black-rat fleas, that swept into England from the Continent and Asia in 1348. It was devastating, particularly as the harvests had failed repeatedly since 1314 and already large areas were unploughed. It is thought that a third of the population died in the first outbreaks. No-one was immune: the Abbot of St Albans, Michael of Mentmore, and 47 of his monks died of the plague in April 1349 alone. The scrawlings give an awesome insight into the state of mind of Ashwell's residents, but the January storms, which did great damage and would have seemed to be the final blow, probably cleared out the plague for a while and gave the community a chance to recover.

Defiant Spike

The church tower, under construction at the time of the plague, is in chalk stone and thus easily incised and carved. There are other equally interesting pieces of graffiti, including a 15th-century drawing of old St Pauls Cathedral in London and, elsewhere in the church, one by a bitter mason or builder which translates 'The corners are not pointed (mortared) correctly – I spit'.

The tower is an immense piece of work – one could speculate that it eventually rose as a defiance or commemoration of the tribulations of the village. At 176ft (54m), it is seen for miles around with its three storeys, massive angle buttresses and crowning 'Hertfordshire spike' spire. Ashwell itself is an exceptionally interesting village. There is a museum in an early 16th-century, timber-framed building, originally built as the local estate office for the Abbey of Westminster, which owned the manor until 1540. Ashwell was a market town and one of five in the county recorded in the Domesday Book. Ashwell's open fields remained unenclosed until as late as 1863. To the west, Caldecote is a deserted, medieval village whose economic viability probably received a serious setback from the Black Death. Owned by St Albans Abbey, it was deserted by 1428 and now consists of just a moated manor house (rebuilt around 1500) and a small church.

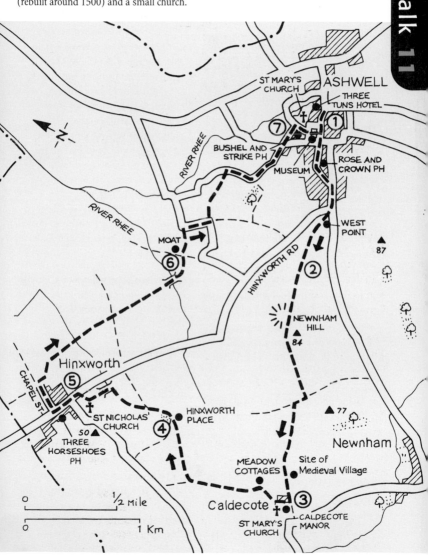

Walk 11 Directions

① Walk west down **Ashwell High Street**, eventually curving left to ascend to a junction. Turn right into **Hinxworth Road**. Shortly after passing the gates to **West Point**, go straight on to a track at a bridleway sign, the road bearing right.

② The track climbs **Newnham Hill** with fine views back to Ashwell church tower and long views northwards. Descend to a bridleway junction. Turn right alongside the hedge, then turn left at a footpath post to go through the hedge and continue westward.

> ### WHERE TO EAT AND DRINK ⓘ
> Ashwell's several pubs include the **Rose and Crown** (also a restaurant) and the **Three Tuns Hotel** in the High Street; also here is the **Thirty One Tea Rooms**. You could try the **Bushel and Strike** in Mill Street. On the route there is the **Three Horseshoes** at Hinxworth.

③ Beyond some former farm cottages turn right on to a concrete road to walk past **Caldecote Manor** and **St Mary's Church** (not open to the public). Follow the road until just before **Meadow Cottages**. Here go left to skirt a copse, then go straight on along a track between fields. When you reach a deep ditch, go left a few paces to cross it. Carry on going straight ahead, aiming for the left end of a hedge, turning right to walk alongside it, and then through pasture.

④ At the lane go straight on past the medieval **Hinxworth Place** to skirt to the right of some scrub. Now go diagonally across some

> ### WHAT TO LOOK FOR ⓘ
> The Black Death that ravaged Ashwell may have fatally weakened nearby **Caldecote**, a small manor of 325 acres (132ha) owned by St Albans Abbey and deserted after 1428. The manor house, church and a cottage incorporating the old rectory are all that remain today. Many villages with 'cold' in their name were deserted in the late Middle Ages. Often they are located in bleak, exposed locations or on poor land.

arable land, heading for **Hinxworth Church**. Go through a hedge to walk alongside a deep ditch and then left over a footbridge. Go along a field edge before turning right into the churchyard via a kissing gate.

⑤ Leave the churchyard along a short lime avenue, turning left to walk up **High Street**, past the quirky war memorial clock tower. Turn right into **Chapel Street**. At a footpath sign go right on to a cinder track which curves left to pass between two cottages, then through vast arable fields. At a crossroads go past some farm buildings to descend across more arable land. Having crossed a footbridge over the **River Rhee**, go diagonally left in a pasture to cross another bridge. Now turn left along the field edge.

> ### WHILE YOU'RE THERE ⓘ
> About 6 miles (9.7km) away from Ashwell, over the border in Bedfordshire, you could round off the day with a trip to the **Shuttleworth Collection** at Old Warden, west of Biggleswade. Started in 1928, it is a superb collection of vintage aircraft and road vehicles, all in airworthy or roadworthy condition.

⑥ At a lane go left past a cottage and opposite go right, with a moat in the field on your left. Turn right on to a lane and, where this turns right, go left, the path curving right through farmland to a stile. Once over this stile turn right and continue along a lane, carrying straight on into **Rollys Lane**.

⑦ At the T-junction go right into **Mill Street** and visit the church. Cross **Swan Street** to the path beside **Ashwell Village Museum**, and back to **High Street**.

From Baldock on the Great North Road

Walk from a Roman and medieval town into the water-meadows along the banks of the River Ivel.

•DISTANCE•	4½ miles (7.2km)
•MINIMUM TIME•	2hrs
•ASCENT / GRADIENT•	95ft (29m)
•LEVEL OF DIFFICULTY•	
•PATHS•	Pavements, lanes and field paths, and stretch of old Great North Road, 1 stile
•LANDSCAPE•	Valley of River Ivel and townscape of Baldock
•SUGGESTED MAP•	aqua3 OS Explorer 193 Luton & Stevenage
•START / FINISH•	Grid reference: TL 099666
•DOG FRIENDLINESS•	On lead in Baldock; some cattle grazing and horse paddocks too
•PARKING•	In High Street, Baldock
•PUBLIC TOILETS•	Old Town Hall on High Street

BACKGROUND TO THE WALK

On the map Baldock looks little more than an appendage to the vast sprawl of Letchworth but the A1(M) bypass that has come between them will at least ensure that the town retains its separate identity. Baldock is very much an ancient town compared with the first 'garden city' of that Edwardian upstart, Ebenezer Howard, begun in 1903. And yet Baldock is similarly an artificial creation, from the Middle Ages, planted at an important crossroads, as was Royston, founded about 1189 further east. Baldock's predecessor, a Romano-British town of some size, grew up where the much older Icknield Way, running north east to south west along the down edge, met the Roman Ermine Street. Another important Roman road from St Albans to the south west joined Ermine Street a little south of the Icknield Way crossroads. The Roman settlement had disappeared well before the medieval town arrived immediately west of its site. The far north of the large parish of Weston reached the Icknield Way and in the 1140s Gilbert, Earl of Clare, gave this area to the Knights Templars. Before 1185 a town had been laid out and Ermine Street and the Icknield Way diverted through the big triangular market place made in Whitehorse Street.

Encroachment

The High Street, running south and wide, was a second market place, but subsequent encroachment has blurred the picture. Encroachment usually happened when a market stall was turned into a permanent shop or structure – it is a universal medieval and Tudor tendency in any market town and can also be seen in St Albans, for example. So the bends on the old A1, which choked the town before the bypass, had their origins when the new town was laid out in the 12th century.

Baldock, amazingly, is a corruption of Baghdad, presumably reflecting the Middle Eastern interests of the Templars, who built the townspeople a sumptuous parish church.

Richard I confirmed the town's charter in 1189. It is interesting to note the tradesmen already listed among the 122 tenants of the 150 acre (61ha) town in a Templars survey of 1185: blacksmith, ironmonger, tailor, shoemaker, tanner, mason, cook, carter, mercer, weaver, saddler, goldsmith, merchant and vintner. Baldock prospered, later playing a key coaching inn role on the Great North Road (which became the A1).

In the 18th century the town acquired fine, brick town houses, particularly along the High Street and Hitchin Street. These were for their prosperous citizens, many of whom were merchants or maltsters, the town having seven maltings. You'll find the older buildings at the north end of the High Street and along the east part of Hitchin Street, Whitehorse Street and Church Street.

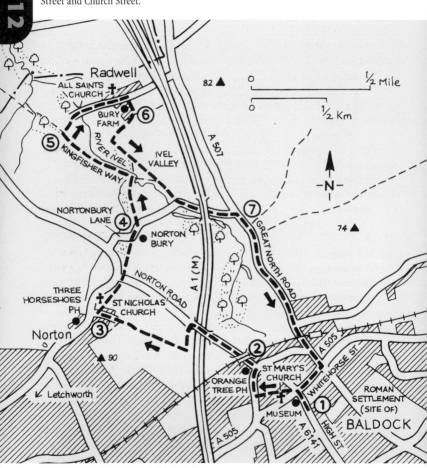

Walk 12 Directions

① Head north along the **High Street** to the crossroads and into **Church Street**, then left into St Mary's churchyard. Pass the church and go left by the church hall, alongside a narrow extension to the churchyard. Emerging on, **Norton Road**, turn right. Beyond the **Orange Tree** pub, turn left.

② Follow Norton Road under the railway. Immediately after the road crosses the **A1(M)** in its cutting go left to a stile with a footpath sign. Turn left along the edge of farmland, with the A1(M) down on your left, and go right on to a grassy path across the arable ground to the right of an electricity pylon. Cross the brow of the hill and descend to a hedge with a pair of cottages to the right of the opening. Through this you reach a lane which leads into old **Norton**. The village has some attractive cottages and the **Three Horseshoes** pub.

③ Turn right through the war memorial lychgate. Go to the right of **St Nicholas' Church** to a gate into a paddock. Follow a hollow trackway and leave via a kissing gate. Cross a lane towards **Nortonbury Lane**, but go to its right, to a footpath which climbs between overgrown hedges to the edge of a field. Descend and turn right on to the lane leading to **Norton Bury farm**.

④ Opposite the stable buildings go to the kissing gate. The path runs diagonally right, through several horse paddocks. Leave these through a kissing gate and turn left, ignoring the iron footbridge over the **River Ivel**. The route now follows the prominantly waymarked **Kingfisher Way** through pasture and water-meadows by the side of the River Ivel.

⑤ Keep on the **Kingfisher Way**, turning right to pass a pink-washed cottage to a lane. Cross the Ivel into **Radwell**. The lane climbs and you now ignore the Kingfisher Way, which turns left. Pass the Victorian **All Saints Church** and go right at a footpath sign by the post box. Walk through the yard of **Bury Farm**.

⑥ At the far end of the farmyard turn right, the path descending past horse chestnuts to the Ivel valley. Turn left at the public footpath sign and walk along a grass path, the river on your right, arable fields on your left. At a road turn left and pass under the **A1(M)**.

⑦ At the main road, the old **Great North Road**, turn right and follow this south into Baldock. At the traffic light crossroads turn right into **Whitehorse Street** and back to **Baldock High Street**.

A View from Deacon Hill

Ascend the chalk downs to Deacon Hill and descend via High Down House.

•**DISTANCE**•	6½ miles (10.4km)
•**MINIMUM TIME**•	2hrs 30min
•**ASCENT / GRADIENT**•	360ft (110m)
•**LEVEL OF DIFFICULTY**•	
•**PATHS**•	Mix of green lanes, tracks and field paths, 1 stile
•**LANDSCAPE**•	Chalk downland, some pasture and some arable
•**SUGGESTED MAP**•	aqua3 OS Explorer 193 Luton & Stevenage
•**START / FINISH**•	Grid reference: TL 146317
•**DOG FRIENDLINESS**•	Good deal of arable land but sheep graze Deacon Hill
•**PARKING**•	On village roads in Pirton
•**PUBLIC TOILETS**•	None on route

BACKGROUND TO THE WALK

The county boundary between Bedfordshire and Hertfordshire is complex along the chalk ridge traversed by the Icknield Way. Despite simplification in the late 19th century, Hexton to the west and Pirton still extend deep into Bedfordshire, sandwiching Shillington, which climbs between them up to Deacon Hill and the Icknield Way. The top of Deacon Hill, just north of the Icknield Way, stands at 567ft (172m) above sea level, giving superb views over the lowlands of Bedfordshire. The land is a Site of Special Scientific Interest (SSSI). Rare chalkland flora and fauna can be found amid its sheep-cropped pasture. Although not as high as the western Chilterns, the chalk hills here between Pirton and west into Bedfordshire are spectacularly cut into by combes and dry valleys. The escarpment presents a deeply corrugated edge, bare or tree-clad, to the claylands below.

Pirton village lies below the chalk hills, in the lowlands whose streams drain north east into the River Hiz near Henlow. The village is centred on Toot Hill, a 12th-century motte and bailey castle. It is one of many so-called 'adulterine' or unlicenced castles that were erected during the Civil Wars of Stephen's reign (1135–54). Their purpose was to offer protection from marauding armies during the anarchy. Toot Hill was built by the de Limesy family, the lords of the manor. Its dismantling, along with many others, was ordered by Henry II after he became King in 1154. There are baileys or ramparted enclosures on each side of the motte – the church is within the east one. 'Toot' means a lookout place, so the mound had a useful later life, although its now only 25ft (7.6m) high. The west bailey is mostly built-up, including the Motte and Bailey pub. South of the castle are other earthworks, one of which is a former lane, Lads Orchard Lane, abandoned in the 19th century. To the west was Chipping Green, now Great Green, so presumably the village had a 'chipping' or market. The church is mostly Norman, but the crossing tower was so dilapidated that, in 1876, it had to be rebuilt in replica. The attractive village has some good examples of timber-framed houses and cottages. These include Walnut Tree Farm, which has a complex of vast, weatherboarded barns that have been converted to houses.

On the downs, ½ mile (800m) south west of Pirton, is High Down House. It was built for the Dockwra family in 1599, then added to in the early 17th century. Picturesque, and set in remnants of parkland, it survived plans to replace it with a Georgian mansion.

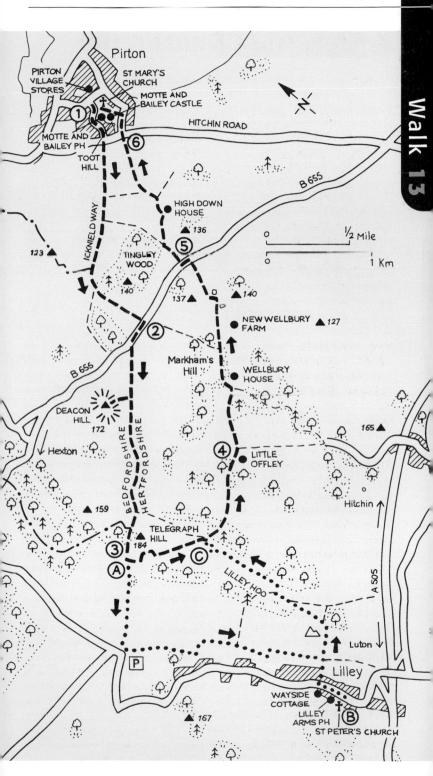

Walk 13 Directions

① Start at St Mary's churchyard in the centre of Pirton. Turn left into **Crabtree Lane**, then **Great Green** with the **Motte and Bailey** pub, to cross the **Hitchin Road** on to a bridleway, the **Icknield Way**. The track climbs steadily between fields, eventually curving left to pass the edge of **Tingley Wood**, now following the county boundary. Past the wood, fork left and continue southwards to the road.

② Turn right, leaving the road, at a lay-by on the left, on to a green lane, here the ancient Icknield Way. At a stile go right to climb **Deacon Hill** through chalk downland and enjoy the wonderful views. The track levels out with woods to the right then descends with downland on the left (**Telegraph Hill**).

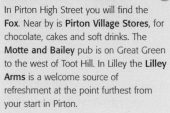

WHAT TO LOOK FOR

Little Offley house, east of The Hoo, is all that remains of a deserted medieval village in the manor of Welles. All you see as you walk past is a wonderfully rambling Tudor mansion, refaced in brick in 1695. According to Sir Henry Chauncy, writing in 1700, the village had 'consisted of divers Houses, as is evident by the Marks of Ancient Foundations, often digg'd up there'.

③ At the bottom of the hill is Point Ⓐ, where Walk 14 diverges. To continue Walk 13 turn left by an information board. The track climbs downland, emerging in open fields. At the crest head towards a solitary oak, then go right, on to a track, turning sharp left on a grass track (Point Ⓒ, where Walk 14 rejoins the route). Head into woodland beside a waymarker following a hedge.

④ Passing **Little Offley** go between two outbuildings, and straight on to a track. Where this bears right, go straight on, heading for Wellbury House, to a lane. Turn left round **Wellbury House** grounds. Follow the track past the drive to **New Wellbury Farm** and **Park View Stables**, going right at a waymarker into a copse. Cross the stables' yard to follow the grassy track uphill. Once through a kissing gate, bear right across meadow to the road.

WHERE TO EAT AND DRINK

In Pirton High Street you will find the **Fox**. Near by is **Pirton Village Stores**, for chocolate, cakes and soft drinks. The **Motte and Bailey** pub is on Great Green to the west of Toot Hill. In Lilley the **Lilley Arms** is a welcome source of refreshment at the point furthest from your start in Pirton.

⑤ Cross the road, go left within the tree belt, then right, signposted to **Pirton**. Cross the field and, through a gate, bear right into pasture, heading towards the chimneystacks of **High Down House**. Follow signs downhill then, through a gate, turn sharp left alongside a hedge. Turn right to follow another hedge to **Hitchin Road**.

⑥ Cross the road into **Walnut Tree Road**, then go left through a kissing gate into pasture. Walk diagonally right to Pirton's church and castle.

WHILE YOU'RE THERE

South east of Pirton, a visit to the historic town of **Hitchin** is most rewarding. It has a long, triangular, medieval market place, which has been substantially encroached and built over. East of the market place is St Mary's Church, mostly rebuilt after an earthquake in 1298. For more information visit the Hitchin Museum and Art Gallery, Paynes Park.

A Gallop to Lilley Hoo

Extend Walk 13 to Lilley and a walk along the ridge of Lilley Hoo.
See map and information panel for Walk 13

•DISTANCE•	9 miles (14.5km)
•MINIMUM TIME•	4hrs
•ASCENT / GRADIENT•	155ft (47m)
•LEVEL OF DIFFICULTY•	

Walk 14 Directions
(Walk 13 option)

Point Ⓐ is at the foot of **Telegraph Hill**. Where Walk 13 turns left, carry on along the Icknield Way downhill, initially with beech trees on both sides. Continue towards a car park and turn left on to a track through arable prairies. Beyond a wood follow the track left, then right. Where it goes left carry straight on, along a path by a hedge.

Cross a lane and continue by the hedge, following it left and descending towards an oak. Turn right, through a gate, into pasture – Lilley Hoo ridge is to your left. Descend alongside a hedge through two fields. At the second gate turn right on to a green lane that climbs gently into **Lilley**.

Turn left and walk uphill, passing a pair of estate cottages, to reach the church, Point Ⓑ. St Peter's, rebuilt in 1871, reused the Norman chancel arch, a couple of 17th-century memorials and a 15th-century piscina from its medieval predecessor. Near by are the **Lilley Arms** and more estate cottages with the Sowerby lion badge on their key-stones.

The Lilley Arms pub has been renamed (at least) twice. In 1806 it was known as the Sugar Loaf, but it had become the Sowerby Arms by the mid-19th century. The Sowerbys were the lords of the manor of Lilley. They lived at Putteridgebury, a mansion about a mile (1.6km) south of the village. They sold the pub in 1907 and it became the Lilley Arms.

Retrace your steps to turn right, opposite **Wayside Cottage**. Follow the green lane across the valley, past the gate passed through earlier, continuing uphill. At the top of the ridge go left signed 'Telegraph Hill'. With woods on your left, continue along the ridge of Lilley Hoo, once noted for horse racing.

At the corner of the second wood turn right at the footpath signposted 'Telegraph Hill, Hollybush Hill' – the track runs across arable fields. Turn left to walk alongside woods, then across more fields, the track now metalled. When you reach a fence corner carry straight on along the track, with the fence and hedge on your left-hand side. Go round a bend but, before reaching a large corner oak tree, go right on a grassy track towards some woodland, rejoining Walk 13 at Point Ⓒ.

Homage to Wallington

A walk along the chalk ridge between George Orwell's home in Wallington and Clothall.

•DISTANCE•	5 miles (8km)
•MINIMUM TIME•	2hrs 15min
•ASCENT / GRADIENT•	130ft (40m) ▲▲▲
•LEVEL OF DIFFICULTY•	🚶🚶 🚶🚶 🚶🚶
•PATHS•	Mainly tracks and green lanes, road in Wallington, 5 stiles
•LANDSCAPE•	Rolling chalk hills, farmland and woods
•SUGGESTED MAP•	aqua3 OS Explorer 193 Luton & Stevenage
•START / FINISH•	Grid reference: TL 291338
•DOG FRIENDLINESS•	Hostile: near Quickswood Farm is warning about rat poison; be careful crossing fast, busy A507 (twice)
•PARKING•	On south side of Kit's Lane, Wallington
•PUBLIC TOILETS•	None on route

Walk 15 Directions

There are two delightful, small villages to enjoy, at the east and west ends of this circuit. The first, Wallington, has a place in literary history, for Eric Blair, better known as George Orwell, bought a cottage here in 1936, and subsequently enjoyed a prolific spell of writing. The second, Clothall, has preserved medieval stained glass paintings of local birds in its church. Your route follows an attractive section of the chalk ridge south of the ancient

WHILE YOU'RE THERE ⓘ

Cromer Windmill – Hertfordshire's only surviving post mill – stands just a mile (1.6km) south of Cumberlow Green. It was built in the early 19th century and was a working mill until 1924. Subsequent decay and loss of sails and machinery was reversed in 1967 when the Hertfordshire Building Preservation Trust acquired it. The Trust had fully restored it with sails by 1991. It is open some afternoons in summer.

Icknield Way, now followed by the A505. The countryside is a wide expanse of rolling arable land in huge fields with few hedges, but the long views to the north make this an exhilarating walk.

Start on **Kit's Lane** at the west end of Wallington. George Orwell lived in a cottage on this street in the late 1930s, after spending time in Lancashire and Yorkshire researching *The Road to Wigan Pier* (published 1937). His thatched and plastered home, The Stores, can be seen to the left of the former Plough pub. Orwell married Eileen O'Shaughnessy in Wallington's parish church, but spent much of his time abroad, first in Spain, fighting in the civil war, and then in Morocco. The couple moved to London in 1940.

Walk uphill, out of the village, then descend to a bridleway to bear left. Now on the Icknield Way path, you wind up and along the chalk ridge, with occasional stretches of hedge.

Walk 15

As it climbs out of a valley the path passes to the left of some modern farm buildings. The track crosses a lane and descends to the busy **A507** Baldock to Buntingford road.

Across the road the path curves along the edge of a field with pasture to your left and the ridge on which Clothall's church stands. Ignore the stile and, at the tree belt, turn left on to a path, which becomes a metalled track. At the village lane turn left and left again after a few paces, through a kissing gate, and uphill to the churchyard. Take time to look at the church, then, from its porch, go down the path towards garages and turn right on to an access drive. At the road turn right. At a bend, just before **Glebe House**, go left at the footpath sign to follow the left edge of a field, uphill. At the top bear right along a track between fields.

WHERE TO EAT AND DRINK ⓘ

There are now no pubs in Wallington. The Derby Arms closed in 1950, while The Plough lasted until as recently as 1988. Clothall is similarly ill-served for its last pub, the Barley Mow, also recently closed down. If you are likely to get peckish on this 5 mile (8km) walk you should purchase 'iron rations' in Baldock or elsewhere en route to the start.

Cross the **A507** and head for a footpath sign pointing you along a track. Past a farmyard the track becomes a green lane heading towards **Clothallbury Woods**. Follow the edge of these woods until the hedge and a tapering tree belt merge from the left. Go diagonally right, downhill to reach a post at the left of some hedges around a pond. Bear left to another footpath sign in front of **Quickswood Farm**.

Turn right (do not cross the footbridge) and walk along the edge of the arable field. At a metalled track go right and pass a cottage to follow the track alongside oak and ash woods. At the corner of the wood go straight on along a green lane with the Corsican pine plantation of **Spital Wood** to your right. Where the track goes right, continue straight on, the footpath now in the edge of the pines, with pheasants everywhere.

Cross a cattle-grazed pasture, heading to the left of some ponds, and go over a stile. Carry straight on. In a shallow dry valley cross a footbridge over a drain. Where the drain goes left, continue straight on. The path crosses a hedged green lane, then a gravelled drive. Continue to the corner of the field, go right over a stile and along a path to **St Mary's Church**. Wallington's church is mainly 15th-century but the chancel was rebuilt in 1864 (badly, according to the guide book).

Out of the churchyard go left to a lane, descend to a junction and turn left to walk down Wallington's Main Street. On the way you will pass **Manor Farm** on the right, whose barn is thought by many to have been the inspiration for the Great Barn featured in George Orwell's *Animal Farm* (1945). Follow the road round by the pillar box and left back into **Kit's Lane**.

WHAT TO LOOK FOR ⓘ

St Mary's Church, in Clothall, is beautifully situated on a ridge that allows fine views to the north and west. In the chancel east window is 15th-century stained glass, notable for the remarkable depictions of birds, including ducks, lapwings, hawks and partridges.

Manners and Mansions at Kingswalden Park

A walk in rolling hills between Preston and Kingswalden with its splendid former deer park.

•DISTANCE•	5 miles (8km)
•MINIMUM TIME•	2hrs 30min
•ASCENT / GRADIENT•	115ft (35m) ▲▲▲
•LEVEL OF DIFFICULTY•	👫 👫 👫
•PATHS•	Mix of field paths, green lanes and village lanes, 5 stiles
•LANDSCAPE•	Rolling arable country and deer park
•SUGGESTED MAP•	aqua3 OS Explorer 193 Luton & Stevenage
•START / FINISH•	Grid reference: TL 180247
•DOG FRIENDLINESS•	Mostly arable land, but sheep graze in Kingswalden Park
•PARKING•	Preston village green, near Red Lion pub
•PUBLIC TOILETS•	None on route

BACKGROUND TO THE WALK

Kingswalden Bury house can be seen from the adjacent churchyard and from the footpath to its north. The deer park is a particularly happy one, sloping from the house into a superb dry valley which means that, as it disappears downhill, the owner could be forgiven for thinking it stretched to infinity. Its grassland, dotted with fine parkland trees – mainly oaks and sweet chestnuts – is now grazed by sheep. Before you reach this part of the park you will have crossed a lime avenue that frames a view to the house's north front.

Modern Mansion

As you look down the lime avenue it would be reasonable to assume you are looking at a Georgian mansion that goes with the park's 18th-century character, but this isn't so. Suprisingly the present Kingswalden Bury house dates from only 1972. The Hale family owned the estate from 1576 until 1884. Their altered and enlarged 17th-century house was drastically recast in Neo-Elizabethan style by the new owners in 1890. It was finally demolished to make way for the current house which was designed by the then leading contemporary practitioners of the revived Georgian or Palladian style, Raymond Erith (1904–73) and Quinlan Terry (1937–). The style is still popular with country house owners. Quinlan Terry's best known solo work is probably the Richmond Riverside complex by the River Thames. In Kingswalden Bury the pair produced a mansion of which Andrea Palladio himself, the great 16th-century Venetian architect, would have been proud. It has pantile roofs and a five-bay centre, with a pediment and two storeys of columns, flanked by simpler two-bay projecting wings. It's a most successful composition, I think, and complements the setting admirably.

Back in Preston you pass the entrance to Princess Helena College, a girls boarding school, which moved here from London in 1935. The gate piers are genuine Georgian ones with 'rubbed', red brick arches to its niches. From the gates you can get a glimpse of the mansion itself, set in Temple Dinsley Park. The Georgian core was built for Benedict Ithell in 1714, but the rest of the building is by Edwin Lutyens and E J Lander who swamped it in 1908–11 and 1935 respectively. The gardens were designed by Lutyens' famous and eccentric collaborator, Gertrude Jekyll. Temple Dinsley gets its name from the Preceptory (a small community) of the Knight's Templar, founded here in 1147 by Bernard Balliol. When the Templars were suppressed in 1312 it passed to the Knights Hospitallers until the Dissolution of the monasteries. A house replaced it in 1540 but was subsequently demolished and only a few stone coffin lids have been dug up over the years.

Walk 16

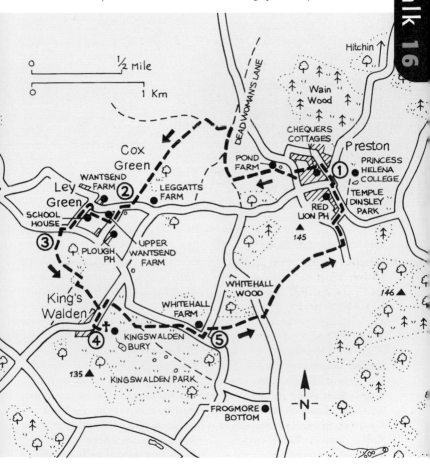

① From Preston village green walk down **Hitchin Road** and turn left into **Chequers Lane**. Beyond **Chequers Cottages** go left at the footpath sign. On reaching a lane go briefly left, then right at another footpath sign, to head diagonally right through pasture. Passing

between a shelter shed and **Pond Farm**, bear left and follow the field path to a kissing gate. Here turn right on to a green lane, called, lugubriously, **Dead Woman's Lane**, the parish boundary between Preston and King's Walden. Follow it uphill to a left turn on to another green lane, which curves left. Follow it downhill. Upon reaching a tarmac lane turn right.

② Near **Wantsend Farm** turn left into **Plough Lane**, which curves uphill. Just before the **Plough** pub go right, over a stile. The path reaches a lane through a children's playground. Out of this turn right to the road, then left past **School House** and left again, signed 'Offley, King's Walden'. At a road junction bear right to a footpath sign beside a de-restriction sign.

③ Turn left on to this footpath, descending alongside the winding hedge. Turn sharp left to pass a modern farm building. Follow the track until it turns left – here your path turns right, along the edge of a wood. Turn left at the next footpath post. At the end of the field turn right, over a stile, into a lane to descend to **King's Walden Church**.

> ### WHERE TO EAT AND DRINK ℹ
> The **Red Lion** in Preston has been a community-owned pub since 1982. The **Plough** at Ley Green is in a house formerly known as Godlets Hall. Both pubs are built of 18th-century red brick.

④ From the churchyard you can glimpse Kingswalden Bury. Retrace your steps uphill, past a fine yew hedge, and at a footpath sign on the right, 'Frogmore Bottom 1' turn right. Now you are in **Kingswalden Park** with views of Kingswalden Bury house's north front. Cross a lime avenue to a superb stretch of deer park. Go diagonally right. Just beyond an oak, at a footpath post, bear left towards a house with a big

> ### WHAT TO LOOK FOR ℹ
> The hamlet of **Cox Green**, west of Preston has a number of impressive, 16th-century farm buildings. First, to the left of the route, Leggatts Farm has a late medieval hall and Tudor cross wing. Turning right you descend to Wantsend Farm with a big four-shaft early 17th-century chimneystack and a Tudor cross wing.

gable, outside the park. Leave the deer park through a kissing gate. Turn right on to a lane. Turn left at the junction past **Whitehall Farm**.

⑤ At a footpath sign go right by a modern farmbuilding, then go diagonally left, descending across some arable land and keeping to the right of **Whitehall Wood**. Across a lane the footpath climbs on a grassy track, then runs alongside hedges and through a horse paddock to reach a lane. Here you turn left. When you reach a junction turn right. At the boundary wall of **Temple Dinsley park**, now home to Princess Helena College, turn left, back to Preston village green.

> ### WHILE YOU'RE THERE ℹ
> Roughly 2 miles (3.2km) east of King's Walden is **St Paul's Waldenbury** or The Bury. Built by Edward Gilbert around 1720, the mansion was altered and then radically recast in 1887 for the Bowes-Lyon family. The Bury was the childhood home of the late Queen Mother. Its superb, 40 acre (16ha) gardens have changed little since they were laid out in the late 1720s. Elements of the gardens include woodland, temples and statues. They are open on some summer Sunday afternoons.

Tewin and the Mimram Water-meadows

A walk from Tewin to the Mimram valley and up to Bramfield, returning via the exquisite Queen Hoo Hall.

•DISTANCE•	6 miles (9.7km)
•MINIMUM TIME•	2hrs 45min
•ASCENT / GRADIENT•	225ft (69m) ▲ ▲ ▲
•LEVEL OF DIFFICULTY•	🚶🚶 🚶🚶 🚶
•PATHS•	Bridleways, field paths through water-meadows, lanes, 2 stiles
•LANDSCAPE•	Rolling chalkland, woodland and water-meadows
•SUGGESTED MAP•	aqua3 OS Explorer 182 St Albans & Hatfield
•START / FINISH•	Grid reference: TL 271156
•DOG FRIENDLINESS•	Cattle graze water-meadows; Tewin Hill has horse paddocks on both sides connected with livery stables
•PARKING•	On roadside around Lower Green, Tewin, opposite Tewin Memorial Hall
•PUBLIC TOILETS•	None on route

BACKGROUND TO THE WALK

Tewin, on a ridge to the north of the River Mimram, probably had its origins in pagan Anglo-Saxon times before AD 600 – the 'Tew' element in the name relates to Tiw, a pagan god (► Walk 22). The village has two greens but the bulk of development has taken place around the Lower Green. The Upper Green is now mainly a sports field and this village can trace over 200 years of cricketing history. Like most Hertfordshire villages, there was no piped water in Tewin until well into the 20th century. On Lower Green you'll find an old well-house, which was converted into a bus shelter in the 1950s.

Earl Cowper's Bricks

Around Lower Green are estate cottages with the 'C' of the landowner Earl Cowper above their dates. One group was built in 1903 and a large memorial hall dates from about 1920. The parish church is out on its own at the end of the ridge with pasture descending to the Mimram valley. To the west of the church stood Tewin House. This was rebuilt around 1717 by General Joseph Sabine, a veteran of the Duke of Marlborough's campaigns against the French who later became Governor of Gibraltar. George I is said to have visited twice, simply to admire the hallway. Sabine died in 1739 and in the church you'll find a superb monument to him, dressed in the costume of a Roman general. Tewin House was pulled down by the 5th Earl Cowper in 1807. It is claimed he salvaged nearly one million bricks from the site and now only stretches of the garden wall survive. The Earl married the daughter of Prime Minister, Lord Melbourne. After the Earl's death, she married again, this time to the Foreign Secretary, Lord Palmerston. Further east, another house took advantage of this picturesque landscape at Marden Hill. Here a 1650s mansion was pulled down in the 1780s and a new one built. This in turn was altered by the great Sir John Soane in 1819.

En route to Bramfield you pass along the edge of Park Wood, certainly a hunting park by 1294. Bramfieldbury, built around 1500, is on its southern margin (hidden behind dense hedges). Like Tewin, Bramfield has many Victorian estate buildings. The shop and post office are in a thatched cottage, which was once the village school. On the green is another well-house, this one was converted into a bus shelter in 1953. But it's after Bramfield that you encounter the greatest building on this route. Queen Hoo Hall is a near perfect late-Elizabethan brick house standing on the ridge ahead with splendid views south. It was built by John Smyth between 1584 and 1589, probably as a hunting lodge. By the end of the 19th century it had become two labourers cottages, but was restored in 1903, and it's worth walking many miles to see such a perfect small mansion.

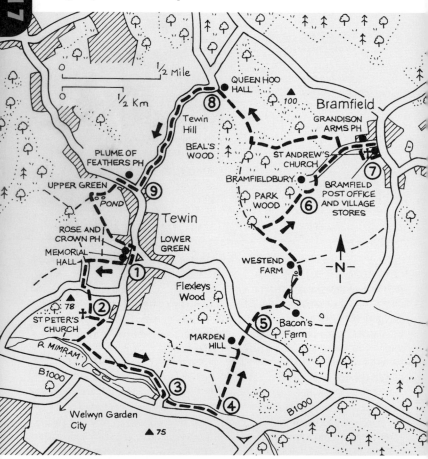

Walk 17 Directions

① From **Lower Green** turn left into **School Lane**, then right at a footpath sign to Digswell. Across some arable fields a track merges from the right. Ignore a footpath crossroads, going next left into a lane. Turn left at a junction and shortly go right to the isolated **St Peter's Church**.

② From the churchyard descend to the valley floor and turn right. The path bears right and then you turn left on to a track. Where it veers left carry straight on, along a field edge to merge with a lane. Keep on this lane to the **River Mimram bridge**.

③ Across the bridge climb a stile on the left to a permissive path in water-meadows alongside the Mimram. At a single-arch bridge cross the river and leave the water-meadows via a kissing gate.

> **WHERE TO EAT AND DRINK** ⓘ
> Both Tewin's pubs serve food. On Lower Green the **Rose and Crown** has been an ale-house since at least 1713. On Upper Green is the **Plume of Feathers**. Bramfield has the **Grandison Arms**. Snacks can be bought at the **Bramfield Post Office and Village Stores**.

④ Go straight across the farmland to enter a scrub belt, becoming parkland to **Marden Hill**. Cross a lime avenue (look left to the mansion) then follow a drive to the road.

⑤ Across the road walk alongside some oak woods. Where the track curves right go straight over a stile into paddocks and out via a kissing gate. Cross more cultivated ground to reach a track. Follow this past the derelict barn of **Westend Farm** to the hornbeams of **Park Wood** and turn right along its edge.

⑥ The path jinks out to pass **Bramfieldbury** (not visible), then cuts across fields to its access lane. Follow this into Bramfield and turn right to the church.

⑦ From Bramfield churchyard turn right into the recreation ground and then left to retrace your steps past the **Grandison Arms** to the valley floor. Here turn right, signposted 'Beal's Wood'. Cross

> **WHAT TO LOOK FOR** ⓘ
> **Tewin Water** is not a lake, but a mainly late 18th-century house that now functions as a school. It had an occupant whose story is told in Maria Edgworth's 1801 novel, *Castle Rackrent*. Married three times already, Lady Cathcart was kidnapped and imprisoned in Ireland for 20 years by her fourth husband. Upon his death she returned to Tewin Water and died in 1789, aged 98.

arable ground to the corner of the wood. The path goes through the woods with occasional waymarker posts. At a track junction briefly join it, then pass a T junction before bearing right to skirt a pheasant enclosure. On reaching more tracks the route takes the second right, on to a wide track. At a pole barrier go right and emerge from the woods on to a track across more cultivated land.

⑧ Pass the superb 1580s **Queen Hoo Hall**. At the lane turn left and follow a winding lane down Tewin Hill into **Tewin**.

⑨ At the main road turn right. Pass the **Plume of Feathers** pub to **Upper Green**, and go left to walk along the edge of the green to a footpath behind scrub. Pass a pond to a metalled green lane and follow this, eventually curving left back to **Lower Green**.

> **WHAT TO LOOK FOR** ⓘ
> Off Tewin's Upper Green you'll find the **Tewin Orchard**. This 70 year old traditional fruit orchard was renewed as part of the village's millennium celebrations. Associated with the site is a 10 acre (4.1ha) nature reserve which teems with wildlife including bats and badgers. Entrance is free and it is open all year round. There is even a hide you can book for evening watching sessions.

Walking the Beane Valley

To Walkern and its castle, then back to Benington.

•DISTANCE•	6 miles (9.7km)
•MINIMUM TIME•	2hrs 45min
•ASCENT / GRADIENT•	165ft (50m) ▲ ▲ ▲
•LEVEL OF DIFFICULTY•	🚶 🚶 🚶
•PATHS•	Field paths, bridleways, village roads, 10 stiles
•LANDSCAPE•	Rolling chalkland scenery, descending to deeply cut valley
•SUGGESTED MAP•	aqua3 OS Explorers 193 Luton & Stevenage; 194 Hertford & Bishop's Stortford
•START / FINISH•	Grid reference: TL 297235 (on Explorer 193)
•DOG FRIENDLINESS•	Mostly arable land but some cattle pasture; horse paddocks round many farms; on leads in Walkern village
•PARKING•	On roadside near Benington's parish church
•PUBLIC TOILETS•	None on route

BACKGROUND TO THE WALK

The River Beane flows south from the chalk ridge that runs north east from Baldock to Royston. This very pretty walk follows the Beane south from Walkern, where it is little more than a meandering stream. The walk's two parishes have a very different relationship to the river. Benington has the river as its western boundary, the village on the chalk plateau to the east, while Walkern extends well to the west with the village on the river, to utilise the water to power its mills.

Different Castles

Walkern's medieval castle stands to the east of the village, at Walkern Bury, on the plateau north of Benington. Both villages' castles were the centre of baronies created by Henry I after 1100 but they were otherwise very different. Hamo de St Clare's Walkern Castle was never more than a motte and bailey type and it's now in paddocks behind Walkern Bury Farm. In contrast, Roger de Valoignes's Benington Castle acquired a stone keep upon its motte mound. Benington Castle had a chequered history, reflecting turbulent times. After the Civil Wars of Stephen's reign (1135–54) it was declared unlicenced by Henry II and demolished in 1177. It was rebuilt by Robert de Valognes, Roger's son and held against Prince John in 1193 for the crusader King, Richard the Lion Heart, who was awaiting a 'King's ransom' in the Duke of Austria's gaol. Resentful Prince John remembered this and in 1213, when he was King, had the castle demolished. Remnants survive, including the keep up to a height of about 9ft (3m) in places. A house called The Lordship, dating from about 1740, can be seen from the churchyard. It occupies much of the bailey of the old castle.

Different Villages

Benington village was once a thriving market town. In 1305 John de Benstede acquired a weekly market and annual fair. The market has since lapsed but the fair still continues. Mostly early 14th century, with a 15th-century tower, St Peter's Church stands to the west of the pretty triangular green, which was formerly the market place. In Walken you'll find more interesting old buildings. Its three pubs span four centuries: the White Lion (partly 16th); the Yew Tree (mid-18th); and the Robin Hood (early 19th). Beyond Stevenage Road, Rooks Nest Farm is an early 17th-century brick farmhouse with a massive central stack and a two-storey porch. There was also a brewery here and maltings, both of which have been converted into housing. At the south end of the village the former Walkers Mill is also now houses, but 'C D Pearman Flour Mills 1881' is still prominently painted on the gable.

Walk 18 Directions

① Walk past the entrance to **Lordship Gardens**. At the green turn left, passing **Old School Green**.

Before a bend go right on to **Bridleway 78**. Go left of the gates to **Walkern Hall**. Passing horse paddocks to your left and the stucco hall to the right, reach a lane and turn right.

Walk 18

② Immediately past **Walkern Hall Farm** turn left to leave the lane for a bridleway signed 'Bassus Green'. Continue past some farm buildings on a track to a stream. Ascend, with woods to your right, curving right to a lane. At the lane go left to **Bassus Green** and straight on at the crossroads, on to a farm access lane.

③ At **Walkern Bury Farm** turn left. At a public bridleway sign go right on to a green lane to descend into the valley bottom. Here you turn left on to a green lane (this is Point Ⓐ, where Walk 19 carries straight on). Follow this muddy green lane into **Walkern** village (Walk 19 rejoins near the church).

④ From the church cross the **River Beane** on a footbridge, then turn left through a kissing gate into pasture. Beyond some farm buildings head diagonally to a kissing gate and thence to the road. Turn left into **Walkern High Street** to walk through the village, passing the school, a former brewery and flour mills.

⑤ Once out of the village, where the road bears left, go over a stile and immediately go left to a gate along a track. Through a kissing gate this is the start of a 1 mile (1.6km) walk along the Beane Valley, the river winding on your left. At a footpath junction, where the river swings right, cross it on a modern footbridge.

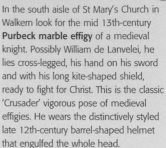

WHAT TO LOOK FOR

In the south aisle of St Mary's Church in Walkern look for the mid 13th-century **Purbeck marble effigy** of a medieval knight. Possibly William de Lanvelei, he lies cross-legged, his hand on his sword and with his long kite-shaped shield, ready to fight for Christ. This is the classic 'Crusader' vigorous pose of medieval effigies. He wears the distinctively styled late 12th-century barrel-shaped helmet that engulfed the whole head.

⑥ Now head between arable fields towards woodlands on the ridge ahead. Cross the road (to a footpath signposted 'Benington 1') and climb to the woods. After these you pass through **Lordship Farm** – follow the waymarker arrows painted on the buildings – on to an often very muddy track. Continue into cattle-grazed pasture. Across a footbridge the path bears right in more pasture to bypass Benington Bury, a large Victorian house, to a stile in the far corner. The path skirts **Lordship Gardens** on your right and sheep pasture on your left to **Walkern Road**. Turn right, back to the green and **St Peter's Church**.

WHERE TO EAT AND DRINK

The **Bell** in Benington has historical interest: an inn by 1693, it has a 16th-century core and an 18th-century hunting scene painted on the chimney breast. Walkern is well provided for with three pubs, the **White Lion**, the **Yew Tree** and the **Robin Hood**, as well as a **general store** and post office.

WHILE YOU'RE THERE

En route you pass the gates to **Benington's Lordship Gardens**. The gardens are usually open between April and September on Wednesday, Sunday and Bank Holiday afternoons. They are well worth visiting, either for the splendid gardens themselves or for the castle remains and the Georgian house. Do not be fooled by the apparently medieval castle gatehouse in flint and stone with 'crumbled' battlements – it is a Picturesque neo-Norman confection of 1832 created for the then owner, George Proctor.

Ardeley's Village Green

Extend Walk 18 to Ardeley with its First World War village green.
See map and information panel for Walk 18

•DISTANCE•	8 miles (12.9km)
•MINIMUM TIME•	3hrs 30min
•ASCENT / GRADIENT•	135ft (41m) ▲▲▲
•LEVEL OF DIFFICULTY•	🚶 🚶 🚶

Walk 19 Directions (Walk 18 option)

From Point Ⓐ, where Walk 18 turns left, the lane continues out of the valley. At the crest go right, the track shortly bearing left, through a tree belt. Continue alongside a hedge with Ardeley's church ahead. Across a valley and stream, the path skirts to the right of a copse.

Here, to the left, you get a glimpse of Ardeley Bury in its parkland. Its battlemented circular flint tower dates from 1820 rather than the Middle Ages. The park dates from the 13th century, while the core of the mansion was built for Sir Henry Chauncey around 1600. However it owes its present romantic medieval appearance to John Murray, the Commissary-General, who remodelled and enlarged the house.

At the road turn right to walk into **Ardeley** village, Point Ⓑ.

The village green has pretty, thatched or tiled and colour-washed cottages. It was created in 1917 for John Howard Carter, the lord of the manor at Ardeley Bury, with help from the local vicar. They first built the long, thatched range of cottages named All Hallows. In 1919 they added the village hall which has a Tuscan columned portico across the green. An octagonal-roofed well-house supplied water. Other cottages round the green were finished by 1920.

Turn right to visit **St Lawrence's Church**. Inside, the nave and aisle roofs are 15th century but the rood loft dates only from 1928.

Out of the church, retrace your steps along the lane. At the war memorial go straight on beside gates, on the footpath signed 'Walkern' through a tree belt and over a stile. Gradually veer right in pasture, away from a fence and chestnut avenue and towards the corner of a wood. Descend to a gate and cross a stream.

The path continues alongside railings, with occasional views of **Ardeley Bury**, before descending to the angle of the field. Go left here, through the tree belt. Continue alongside a hedge on a grass margin. Where a footpath joins from the left go right through a shelter belt to a gate. Go round two sides of a paddock to a path alongside the churchyard to the lane into **Walkern**. Turn right to rejoin Walk 18 at Point Ⓒ.

Towers and Battlements Around Knebworth

A walk in and around Knebworth Park with its Gothic mansion.

•DISTANCE•	5 miles (8km)
•MINIMUM TIME•	2hrs 20min
•ASCENT / GRADIENT•	90ft (27m)
•LEVEL OF DIFFICULTY•	
•PATHS•	Paths and tracks, 4 ladder stiles, 7 stiles
•LANDSCAPE•	Parkland in gentle rolling hills cut by dry valleys
•SUGGESTED MAP•	aqua3 OS Explorer 193 Luton & Stevenage
•START / FINISH•	Grid reference: TL 218213
•DOG FRIENDLINESS•	Herds of deer and high ladder stiles distinctly dog-unfriendly, also sheep in fields around Burleigh Farm
•PARKING•	Lay-by on B656 between Codicote and Langley, ½ mile (800m) south of Langley
•PUBLIC TOILETS•	None on route

Walk 20 Directions

Knebworth is as well-known nowadays for its open air rock concerts as for its extraordinary country house, decked out in the 19th century with a profuse Gothic and Tudor style re-working. This walk takes in the house, together with the parkland, roamed by herds of red and sika deer.

From the lay-by on the **B656** walk south to the footpath sign. Turn left on to the hedged farm access road to **Burleigh Farm**, a rambling 16th-century timber-framed house with massive chimneystacks. Before its yard go left over a stile into sheep pasture and continue past a copse to a stile. A grass path crosses arable land to a hornbeam and oak wood. Turn left to follow the wood to the road, reached via steps. Cross the road and descend to cross a stile, then head towards a gate,

skirting the edge of a copse. At the gate go left, around a pond. Head to a stile to cross pasture (hornbeam woods to your left). Now go over a stile to walk alongside some arable land to a lane by the 18th-century **Rusling End Cottage**. Turn left along the lane to a wood. Go left at the footpath sign to follow the track into the woods. On reaching a footpath post go right to leave the track. Occasional footpath posts guide you through the woods, eventually joining a track that leads out, over a footbridge, to the **B656**.

Cross the road to a tall ladder stile and into **Knebworth Park**. Over a stream go straight on uphill alongside a deer fence. Cross the drive and, to the right, you have a view of **Tower Lodges**, formed in 1816 from demolished parts of the Tudor mansion. Go over another ladder stile. Head diagonally left to pass to the right of the **Cenotaph** column, erected in memory of

Walk 20

Elizabeth Bulwer Lytton who died in 1842. A lime avenue frames views of the mansion.

Continue downhill to another ladder stile. Follow the path to a road. Cross into **Slip Lane**. Past **Slip Cottage** turn left at a footpath sign. Trek across cultivated land, heading for two oak trees to the right of a close of modern vernacular-style houses. Continue alongside their rear boundary, then go over a stile and proceed straight on, through an orchard garden, then left along a narrow path to the road.

At the small, triangular green turn right into **Park Lane**. Just before some housing go left, passing a children's playground, then through a kissing gate into horse paddocks. Leave through a kissing gate and turn left, still with woodland to your left. Cross a dry valley (with arable ground to your right) to a road. Once over this go through a high kissing gate, beside a pretty lodge, back into **Knebworth Park**.

The route heads for the parish church and gives good views of the north east front of Knebworth House. It was built as a courtyard house, probably around 1500, by William Lytton, who was Sheriff of Hertfordshire and Essex in 1511. The buildings around three sides of this courtyard were demolished in 1811 and 1813. The remodelling was partly for Elizabeth Bulwer Lytton and partly for Edward

Bulwer Lytton, the novelist, playwright and MP. He inherited the property in 1844 and made further alterations. As you will see the result is extraordinary and complex. A confusion of turrets and battlements, all in Tudor style, decidedly un-academic but tremendous fun.

The very worthwhile and interesting parish church is basically Norman with a west tower built in 1420 for Sir John Hotoft, of Knebworth Park. Inside, its chief glories are the monuments in the Lytton Chapel, including two by the great sculptor Edward Stanton commemorating William Lytton (1705) and Sir George Strode (1710).

From the churchyard head towards the **Barns Banqueting Centre**. Turn right at a crossroads into a lime avenue to descend to the valley floor. At the T-junction go straight on to some woods, then turn left along their edge. At a footpath post go right, still alongside the deer fence. Cross a dam and go out over another ladder stile. Bear right with footpath posts guiding you out of the woods, then go straight on, along a grassy path between arable fields. At a stile go left around two sides of a paddock on a permissive path, bypassing Burleigh Farm. When you reach the farm access road turn left to walk back to the main road and the lay-by.

Royal Hunting Days at Hunsdon

A walk through the former parkland of Hunsdon House, a great royal estate, to the Stort Valley and back.

•DISTANCE•	6 miles (9.7km)
•MINIMUM TIME•	2hrs 30min
•ASCENT / GRADIENT•	150ft (46m) ▲ ▲ ▲
•LEVEL OF DIFFICULTY•	🚶 🚶 🚶
•PATHS•	Trackless arable ground, paths, canal tow path, verges and pavements
•LANDSCAPE•	Undulating London clay country on borders of Essex
•SUGGESTED MAP•	aqua3 OS Explorer 194 Hertford & Bishop's Stortford
•START / FINISH•	Grid reference: TL 417140
•DOG FRIENDLINESS•	On lead near busy A414 and other roads; some livestock-free, arable countryside
•PARKING•	Along High Street, Hunsdon, near and west of Crown pub
•PUBLIC TOILETS•	None on route

BACKGROUND TO THE WALK

This walk focuses on the great estate of Hunsdon, whose glory days were in the Tudor age. The poorly-drained boulder clay hereabouts proved ideal for the semi-wild hunting park landscape favoured in medieval and Tudor times. A hunting park was made here after the Norman Conquest. Its earliest known royal connection dates from 1445, when Richard, Duke of York, was permitted to enlarge the park. In 1447 he was licensed to build a tower of stone and crenellate it, royal consent being needed to construct any battlements. However, that year the estate passed to Sir John Oldhall, who duly built the mansion with a tower 100ft (30m) high by 80ft (24m) square.

Stag Party

By 1527 the house and estate were owned by Henry VIII. He increased the number of hunting parks to three and is recorded as personally killing two stags there in 1532. He spent a great deal of money on Hunsdon House, the shape being an early example of the 'E-plan'. When Elizabeth I granted the estate to Sir Henry Carey in 1559 it must have been a very substantial mansion. Carey, who took the title Baron Hunsdon, was one of the Queen's most important advisors. A blunt and direct soldier, a jouster, Governor of Berwick and Privy Councillor, he was Elizabeth's first cousin. His mother was Mary Boleyn, sister of the Queen's mother, Ann Boleyn. There is a famous painting of the Queen arriving in procession at a very fanciful Hunsdon in about 1580. This was truly the golden age of Hunsdon House for in 1653, after the Civil War, the Royalist Lord Hunsdon had to sell the estate. The Hertfordshire brewing family, the Calverts, set out to rebuild the house but faltered, and the centre and south wings were demolished in 1804. The present house, three storeys high and battlemented, is based around the 1447 structure and the Tudor north wing. Most of the external walls incorporate original brickwork, as far as the middle of the second storey.

Ploughed Under

The park is now a shadow of it former self, just a small area near the house, the remainder has gone under the plough. Near the start of the walk is Hunsdon Lodge Farm, the lodge in question was demolished in 1946. It may have been a hunting lodge in the northernmost of the three royal parks but now is amid cloying arable farmland and an old Second World War airfield. You get a partial view of Hunsdon House from the parish churchyard. The church itself, well to the south of the village, has notable monuments and a sumptuous Jacobean screen into the south chapel. Both this chapel and the north one are in Tudor brick, while the rest is in flint with stone dressings from the early and late 15th century.

Walk 21 Directions

① Walk east along the **High Street**. At the parish pump bear right into **Drury Lane**. At its end go through the gates to the **Gilston Park Estate**, then straight ahead on a farm access track between arable fields and the remnants of a lime avenue. The path skirts to the left of **Hunsdon Lodge Farm**, then runs through more cultivated fields, bearing right to cross a track and enter woodland. Once out of the woods cross a concrete road (a copse to your right), then go straight on across more cloying ground.

② Halfway across this field, at a waymarker post marking a T-junction of footpaths, turn right and descend the arable prairie to a track. Cross this and head for the right-hand end of a vestigial hedgerow. Here, thankfully, you join a track which becomes a green lane. It descends, with a stream shortly appearing alongside. At a lane turn right by a footpath sign to Acorn Street and Hunsdon. Just before **Eastwick Hall Farm** turn left over a stile by a footpath post.

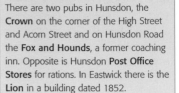

WHERE TO EAT AND DRINK

There are two pubs in Hunsdon, the **Crown** on the corner of the High Street and Acorn Street and on Hunsdon Road the **Fox and Hounds**, a former coaching inn. Opposite is Hunsdon **Post Office Stores** for rations. In Eastwick there is the **Lion** in a building dated 1852.

WHILE YOU'RE THERE

To see a remarkable survival with rich historic overtones visit the **Rye House Gatehouse** next to the River Lea. This battlemented brick gatehouse is all that remains of a moated courtyard mansion, licenced in 1443, and famous for being the scene of the Rye House Plot of 1683 which schemed the assassination of Charles II. It is best reached via Stanstead Abbotts, along the west side of the river.

③ Descend alongside a hedge. By the pylon bear left on a track that winds to the road. The horse-grazed paddocks on each side contain the earthworks of **Eastwick Manor**, which burnt down in the 1840s.

④ At the lane turn right and descend to a crossroads, by the pub and the church, in **Eastwick** village. Go along **Eastwick Road** (with the **Lion** on your right). Follow the lane to the **A414** and cross this with

care. Now take a lane that crosses the **River Stort** on a ford bypass footbridge. Continue to the **Lee and Stort Navigation**.

⑤ At **Parndon Mill Lock** cross the lock bridge and turn right on to the canal tow path. Follow this for about a mile (1.6km). Cross the canal again at **Hunsdon Lock**, then double back to a gate in order to cross a single-arch, concrete bridge over the mill leet.

⑥ Follow the lane uphill to cross the **A414** dual carriageway again. Follow the Hunsdon road (verges mostly on the right hand side). The many trees in the grounds of **Hunsdon House** appear on the right and then **St Dunstan's Church**. Behind the churchyard you can get a glimpse of Hunsdon House itself.

⑦ Continue along the road, a pavement soon appearing on the right-hand side. The main road bears right into **Acorn Street**. Follow this as it winds back into **Hunsdon** village.

WHAT TO LOOK FOR

Eastwick village, virtually rebuilt for Lord Hunsdon's estate, has several dated buildings around its crossroads, built in a Tudor style; the Lion pub in 1852, estate cottages of 1861 and 1872 and a school of 1884. The church was also rebuilt by the estate in the 1870s. In its churchyard is one of those poignant reminders of the impact of war on a small village – the grave of a local Home Guardsman killed in October 1940 by the same bomb that mortally wounded his father, an Air Raid Warden.

Ermine Street Heroes and Turnpike Road Pioneers

From a pagan settlement at Thundridge to stories of 20th-century heroism at High Cross.

•**DISTANCE**•	4 miles (6.4km)
•**MINIMUM TIME**•	2hrs
•**ASCENT / GRADIENT**•	140ft (43m) 🔺🔺🔺
•**LEVEL OF DIFFICULTY**•	🚶 🚶 🚶
•**PATHS**•	Good paths and tracks with only one large arable field to cross, no stiles
•**LANDSCAPE**•	Valleys and chalk hills, a mix of arable land and pasture
•**SUGGESTED MAP**•	aqua3 OS Explorer 194 Hertford & Bishop's Stortford
•**START / FINISH**•	Grid reference: TL 359172
•**DOG FRIENDLINESS**•	Sheep pasture and horse paddocks along Rib Valley
•**PARKING**•	Ermine Street, Thundridge (to east of A10)
•**PUBLIC TOILETS**•	None on route

BACKGROUND TO THE WALK

Although Thundridge and Wadesmill are on Roman Ermine Street, they were not always so. Thundridge, like many early Anglo-Saxon settlements, grew up off the road, about ¹⁄₂ mile (800m) to the east along the valley of the River Rib. Of this original village only the 15th-century tower of the old church, romantically situated overlooking the river in a tree-filled churchyard, survives. There is a reset Norman doorway in its tower arch, together with the remains of a moat and a fragment of the old manor house, Thundridge Bury. This peculiar fragment is the Tudor chimneystack with three fireplaces one above the other. The rest of the house was demolished in 1811.

Pagan God
The name 'Thundridge' refers to Thunor, a pagan Anglo-Saxon god, and dates the first settlement to before about AD 600, that is, before the East Saxons were converted to Christianity. The new St Mary's Church was built in 1853 and is dominant on the crest of the ridge by Ermine Street. It's a stiff climb up from the River Rib bridge, which was designed by Caleb Hatch in 1825 but has modern balustrades.

War Hero
In Marshalls Lane, High Cross, you'll see Marshalls, a Victorian brick house on the left. This was once the home of Colonel Arthur Martin-Leake. He was an army surgeon, who held the distinction of having been awarded the Victoria Cross twice (known as 'VC and Bar'). Born in 1874, his first act of meritorious bravery was at Vlakfontein, South Africa in 1902, during the Boer War. Despite being under heavy fire from Boer positions, he continued to dress men's wounds, even after he had been shot himself. His second Victoria Cross came in Belgium in 1914, during the First World War. Again Martin-Leake managed to tend to injured men despite constant enemy fire from nearby trenches. He was the first to receive

the medal twice and remains one of only three to have been recognised in this way. In the Second World War he took command of a local Air Raid Precautions unit. He died in 1953 and is buried at St John's Church, High Cross.

Wadesmill is the site of the first road toll-house in England. The turnpike was authorised by an Act of Parliament in 1663. The income it generated was to be used to repair and keep open the roads. The local malting industry was mainly responsible, since their laden wagons churned up the local highways. There was no actual toll gate at this stage – one was not installed until many years later. A little up the hill on the west side of Ermine Street is an obelisk erected in 1879 in memory of Thomas Clarkson, a Quaker from Wisbech, who in 1785 'resolved to devote his life to bringing about the abolition of the slave trade'. It was placed here by Arthur Giles Pullar of Youngsbury.

Walk 22 Directions

① At the bend in **Ermine Street** there are two footpath signs: follow the 'Ware' one steeply uphill to the Victorian parish churchyard, for good views northwards and westwards. Retrace your steps downhill to Ermine Street and follow the other footpath, signposted 'Thundridge Old Church'. After a kissing gate go straight on across pasture, now on

WHAT TO LOOK FOR ⓘ
The main local land-owning family, the Hanburys, left their mark on Thundridge village. At the 'new' church, a **tomb** by the gate is a sad indication of 19th-century infant mortality. Robert and Emily Hanbury buried five of their children in the churchyard between 1825 and 1834. Down the hill on old Ermine Street, you will see a long row of **gabled brick cottages**, built by the Hanburys for their estate workers between 1864 and 1901, and the village school built in 1894.

the **Hertfordshire Way**, then cross some arable land to descend to the Rib Valley. Turn right on to a lane. Where it goes right carry straight on on to a metalled track. The ruined church tower is visible ahead and to the left, beyond the river, are the grounds of **Youngsbury**, a country house from 1745 set in 'Capability' Brown parkland.

② Only the tower of the medieval parish church remains, the rest having been pulled down in 1853. Continue along the metalled track, between pastures. Where the track goes right, continue straight ahead, now on a footpath. Cross an access road. At a footpath crossroads go left over a footbridge that bypasses the River Rib ford.

③ Now climb out of the valley with arable fields to your right, Youngsbury's Picturesque parkland to your left. At the brow the track skirts woodland, in fact an arboretum. Carry straight on, ignoring the track bearing right. Go straight on, past some farm buildings. The track, now metalled, curves left and downhill.

④ By some white-painted, iron gates go sharp right across cultivated land, heading for a footpath post in front of some woods. Turn left here and head west towards the tower and spirelet of **High Cross Church**.

⑤ From the churchyard turn left down the **A10**, here following the course of **Ermine Street**. Near the **White Horse** pub turn right into **Marshall's Lane**. Pass some modern houses, then **Marshall's Farm** and **Marshall's** (both Victorian), to descend into the valley by a winding holloway lane.

WHILE YOU'RE THERE ⓘ
If Victorian churches are not to your taste head 4 miles (6.4km) north west to Little Munden. Here **All Saints Church** sits on its hill in a parish of scattered 'Ends' or hamlets known locally as Little Devon for its winding high-banked lanes. A part-Norman church, its chief glories are the superb tombs of Sir John Thornbury, died 1396, and his son, Sir Philip, died 1456, and their wives.

⑥ Cross **The Bourne** and go left by the footpath signposted 'Wadesmill' (the footpath is to the left, not the field track on the right). The path keeps alongside The Bourne almost into Wadesmill where it crosses to the other bank on a footbridge. It becomes a gravelled access lane and you reach the **A10** road.

⑦ Turn right over the **River Rib** bridge. Turn left at the **Post Office Stores** of 1904, back into **Ermine Street**, Thundridge.

WHERE TO EAT AND DRINK ⓘ
The **White Horse** is at the crossroads in High Cross. In Wadesmill the **Feathers Inn** is on the left and the **Anchor** is on the right, past the B158 junction. All three serve food. On the Thundridge side of the River Rib the **Post Office Stores** has chocolate, snacks and drinks.

Ware and Hertford Towns

From the maltings town of Ware to the county town of Hertford.

•DISTANCE•	6 miles (9.7km)
•MINIMUM TIME•	2hrs 45min
•ASCENT / GRADIENT•	100ft (30m)
•LEVEL OF DIFFICULTY•	
•PATHS•	Town streets, field and riverside paths, 1 stile
•LANDSCAPE•	Two townscapes, water-meadows, woods and river cliffs
•SUGGESTED MAP•	aqua3 OS Explorer 194 Hertford & Bishop's Stortford
•START / FINISH•	Grid reference: TL 360142
•DOG FRIENDLINESS•	On leads in towns; should find company in water-meadows
•PARKING•	Kibes Lane car park, off High Street, Ware
•PUBLIC TOILETS•	By car park, Ware; by Castle, Hertford

BACKGROUND TO THE WALK

The strategic, if not economic, importance of Hertford can be seen in the remains of its Royal castle. However the town has Anglo-Saxon origins, well before this feudal castle arrived in 1067. During the re-conquest of the Danelaw by King Edward the Elder (ruled AD 899–924), the son of Alfred the Great, this settlement at a ford across the River Lea emerged into written history. The *Anglo-Saxon Chronicle* records of AD 913: 'In this year, after Martinmas (11 November), King Edward had the more northerly fortress at Hertford built, between the Mimram and the Beane and the Lea. Another part of his forces built the fortress at Hertford meanwhile on the southern bank of the Lea.' The latter is now Hertingfordbury, 'bury' being from the Anglo-Saxon 'burh' or defended town.

However the northern burh, Hertford, actually on the river, prospered while Hertingfordbury remains a small village. By 1011 the burh had become the centre of an administrative area, the county or shire of Hertfordshire. It also had two market places, a mint for coinage and its own town 'reeve', a high official seen as a forerunner to the mayor. When the Normans conquered England Hertford received its castle, initially a motte (earth mound) and bailey type. These were the best days economically as soon nearby Ware on Ermine Street rapidly overtook Hertford. Indeed bitter rivalry between the two towns often spilt over into violence. Although Hertford kept its county town status, by 1338 its taxable value was half that of Ware.

Of Hertford's castle the motte survives to a height of 22ft (6.7m). There is also some 12th-century curtain walling, but the most impressive surviving structure is the three-storey, brick gatehouse built for Edward IV in the 1460s. The castle's most famous military event was its capture after a 25-day siege in 1216 by Prince Louis, the Dauphin of France.

Our route visits several of Hertford's other sights: Parliament Square, laid out only in 1821; James Adam's former Shire Hall of 1769; the Salisbury Arms (formerly the Bell) of 1570; and the blue-coat Christ's Hospital School, which was founded in London by Edward VI for poor children – the juniors moved here in 1683. At Bengeo (before you reach Hertford) the parish church is a rare, virtually intact Norman one with nave, chancel and semi-circular east apse. It has an attractive 18th-century brick porch, evidence of an anchorite or hermit's cell, and some 13th-century wall paintings.

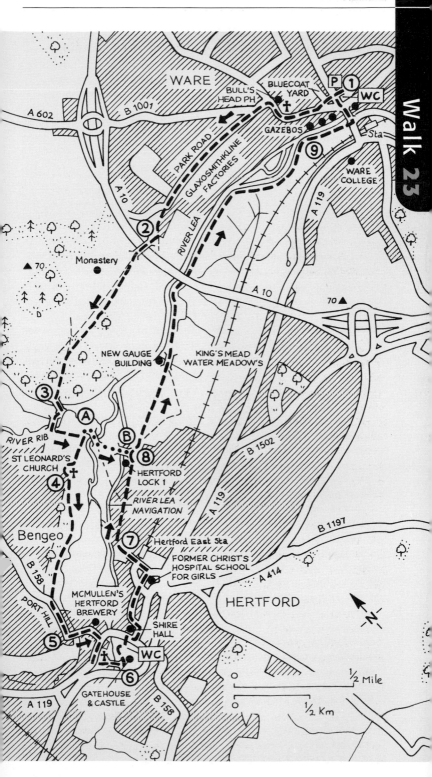

Walk 23 **Directions**

① From the car park walk down **East Street**, past the entrance to **Bluecoat Yard**, to merge with **High Street**. Past the Town Hall and church, the road curves right into **Baldock Street**. At the roundabout turn left into **Watton Road**, then straight on along **Park Road** past GSK. Go straight on at a fork.

② Cross the **A10 bridge** to a lane. At a gap by a waymarker go left, parallel to the lane in lime avenue remnants. Across pasture carry straight on, into woodland, shortly bearing left to descend to the valley.

> **WHAT TO LOOK FOR** ⓘ
> The former **Christ's Hospital School for Girls** moved in 1985 to join the boys near Horsham, but the complex of buildings remains. The earlier ones are linked by an avenue flanked by dormitory blocks, now flats. The oldest structure is the Stewards House and School Hall, built in 1695.

③ At a lane go left across a bridge and bear right along a lane, the river to your left. Once across the river bridge go immediately left over a stile, heading for the **River Lea bridge**. Walk 24 crosses the bridge (Point Ⓐ), but this walk goes right, climbing from the valley towards a house in **Benego**.

④ After visiting Bengeo's Norman church, continue westwards, downhill, past a cottage called **The Vineyard**. Keep on this path to ornamental gates, then turn left on to **Port Hill**, now in Hertford.

⑤ Go downhill, then bear left into **Cowbridge**. Cross the river, pass **McMullen's Brewery**, and turn

right into **St Andrew Street**. Past the church go left on a footpath. Cross a footbridge then turn left through a gate by a playground, into **Hertford Castle**'s grounds.

> **WHERE TO EAT AND DRINK** ⓘ
> Ware and Hertford have a wide range of pubs, restaurants and cafés. If you want historic buildings to accompany your refreshment try the **Salisbury Arms Hotel**, opposite Shire Hall in Hertford or the 16th-century **Bull's Head** in Baldock Street, Ware.

⑥ Cross a stream and turn left to walk past the gatehouse and go out between gate-piers. Turn right to **Parliament Square**. Turn left into **Fore Street**, then left again into **Market Street**. Next, turn right past the **Duncombe Arms**. Go straight on across **Bircherley Green** towards a store through **Bluecoat Yard**. Turn left to pass the station forecourt.

⑦ Carry on into **Dicker Mill**. Go right before the bridge to the tow path. Follow this to **Hertford Lock 1** (Point Ⓑ on Walk 24).

⑧ Go through the gate and head left towards a bridge. Cross it and go left to the **New Gauge building**. Through the gate turn right to follow the **Lee Navigation** under the A10 and on into **Ware**.

⑨ Passing the **gazebos**, ascend to the modern road bridge and turn left back into town.

> **WHILE YOU'RE THERE** ⓘ
> Although only open occasionally, **Scott's Grotto**, within Ware College, is a fascinating and romantic 'artificial cave'. It has passages linking small chambers, their walls are lined with flints, shells and glass fragments. It was built for John Scott of Amwell House.

Ware Abouts

Shorten Walk 23 to focus on the historic malting town of Ware.
See map and information panel for Walk 23

•DISTANCE•	4 miles (6.4km)
•MINIMUM TIME•	2hrs
•ASCENT / GRADIENT•	100ft (30m)
•LEVEL OF DIFFICULTY•	

Walk 24 **Directions** (Walk 23 option)

From Point Ⓐ, where Walk 23 turns right at the river bank to climb to **Bengeo**, cross the river footbridge. Turn left, across the flat valley towards the **River Lee Navigation** and the lock bridge by **Hertford Lock 1**. Over it rejoin Walk 23 at Point Ⓑ by the gate into King's Mead water-meadows.

This is the largest area of grazed flood-meadows in Hertfordshire. In its 247 acres (100 ha) you could expect to see delicate, white meadow saxifrage, deep pink pyramidal orchids and delicate adders-tongue ferns.

An Act of Parliament in 1739 authorised the canalisation of the River Lea, largely to facilitate the transport of malt and corn to London from the rich country of east Hertfordshire that fed the malting industries of Ware and Bishop's Stortford. The River Lee Navigation was a great boon as the heavy malt and corn wagons, toiling behind their six- or eight-horse teams, had long made Hertfordshire's roads virtually impassable. Shortly after its completion, Ware was sending over 5,000 quarters (1,270 tonnes) of malt and corn to London in barges. By the mid-19th century Ware had well over 70 maltings. Quite a few of them survive, either empty or with new uses, such as that behind Kibes Lane car park, now Waggers Function Room.

As you approach Ware bridge along the Lee Navigation tow path, note the numerous small, square garden rooms or gazebos, by or overhanging the river. They are mostly weatherboarded with Georgian sash windows and tiled, pyramidal roofs. These were built by prominent maltsters whose houses along the south side of the High Street had long plots running down to the river. No doubt this strategic location allowed them to admire their laden barges as they passed on their way to London.

Ware itself is a fine town with a high survival rate of 16th- and 17th-century, timber-framed buildings from its earlier prosperity, as well as Georgian and later buildings from the malt and corn boom. It was granted a market charter in 1199 and an annual fair in 1254. With its huge medieval parish church, the town is well worth a longer visit.

Walk 25

Elizabethan North Mymms Park

From Brookmans Park Station walk across country to North Mymms.

•DISTANCE•	4 miles (6.4km)
•MINIMUM TIME•	2hrs
•ASCENT / GRADIENT•	75ft (23m)
•LEVEL OF DIFFICULTY•	
•PATHS•	Field paths, tracks, lanes, 11 stiles
•LANDSCAPE•	Pastoral stream valley, hills, woods and parkland
•SUGGESTED MAP•	aqua3 OS Explorer 182 St Albans & Hatfield
•START / FINISH•	Grid reference: TL 241040
•DOG FRIENDLINESS•	Sheep pasture and ponies
•PARKING•	Car park east of Brookmans Park railway station
•PUBLIC TOILETS•	None on route

Walk 25 Directions

The opening of Brookmans Park Station in 1926 spawned rapid growth of its suburb to the east. The new buildings occupied much of the park to a mansion that had burnt down in 1891 – its stables are now a golf club house. Fortunately the railway line also served as a barrier to westward development and our walk is in this unspoilt area, focusing on North Mymms Park, an Elizabethan mansion, set in wonderful parkland. At its gates, the parish church feels more like a private chapel.

Cross the railway bridge from the Brookmans Park side and follow **Station Road** downhill as far as the left turn, **Bradmore Lane**. Here a footpath sign doubles back parallel to Station Road.

The path descends to the valley floor, an unkempt hedge on the left and a chain-link fence on the right.

Here cross a footbridge and stile, turning right alongside a post-and-net fence; a stream, often dry, is beyond. (You may see ponies grazing amid the sheep.) At the corner of the field go right, over a stile, then, in a few paces, go left over another at the corner of **Brick Kiln Wood**. Keep on the path, the stream now to the left with views of the Royal Veterinary College beyond. Past the woods and near the end of an arable field, the path goes left to cross the stream-bed, then winds through scrub to another bridge, over the **Mimmshall Brook**.

Across the bridge turn left along a lane. Opposite **Hawkshead Lane**, with its two-arch bridge over the

> **WHERE TO EAT AND DRINK** ⓘ
>
> There is a choice at the hamlet of Water End, ½ mile (800m) east of St Mary's Church in North Mymms Park. The **Waterend Café** is open Monday to Friday in the mornings or, a little down Woodgate Road, is the **Woodman** pub.

Walk 25

brook, go right. At the main road turn left for perhaps 60yds (55m), before crossing to the footbridge over the **A1(M)**. Over the footbridge descend and turn sharp right to walk alongside the A1(M) on a metalled track, soon bearing left uphill. Over the crest the track descends past a rendered, octagonal structure, a former well-house. Beyond, the metalled track goes right at an ancient oak while our route goes straight on along a green lane. Continue straight over a footpath crossroads, heading to the right-hand side of oak, sweet chestnut and hornbeam woods. Over a stile walk alongside the woods and, over another stile, turn right on to a metalled track which joins an access drive to **North Mymms Park**.

On your left is a dense, holly hedge that prevents anything more than glimpses of the mansion grounds, here something of an arboretum. At the drive junction go left to the church. Here too is the remnant of the medieval village cleared for the park, the timber-framed **Church Cottage** and the late 17th-century, former vicarage. In the mainly 14th-century church the most interesting monument is that in the chancel. It was sculpted by the fashionable Peter Scheemakers for Lord Somers, Chancellor to William III. A figure of Justice sits above an unusual marble doorway which once led to his vault.

To the west of the church tower a kissing gate and stile lead into the park. Heeding the warnings about bulls loose in the fields, head right to cross the drive and get good views of North Mymms Park mansion. Built by Sir Ralph Coningsby in the early 1590s,

it's a typical Elizabethan great house with vast, stone mullioned and transomed windows and parapetted gables. It was built in red brick with diamond-shaped patterns in blue brick, and with clusters of tall chimneys. The mansion decayed in the 17th century but was restored several times, and then was thoroughly re-Elizabethanised in the 19th century.

Retrace your steps through the churchyard to the drive. Turn right and then left through a gate into pasture, aiming for the footbridge over the A1(M). The path skirts the corner of a cricket pitch and then heads for a stile to the left of an electricity pole. Over this, turn right to cross the motorway.

Descend to the road and cross to the **Waterend Café**, turning left past an engineering company on to a tarmac footpath alongside the road. Shortly past a concrete bridge parapet, descend to a stile on the edge of a copse. Follow the path, which winds through a scrubby copse, until you emerge on the edge of an arable field. Carry on along its edge, the field to your left, bearing right, downhill, to a lane gate. Turn left along the lane to a T-junction. Turn right into **Station Road** and back to **Brookmans Park**.

Around Little Berkhamsted

A walk on the ridges south of the Lea between Little Berkhamsted and Essendon villages.

•DISTANCE•	4 miles (6.4km)
•MINIMUM TIME•	2hrs
•ASCENT / GRADIENT•	195ft (59m)
•LEVEL OF DIFFICULTY•	
•PATHS•	Bridleways, field paths and golf course, 7 stiles
•LANDSCAPE•	Ridges and valleys, pine trees around golf course
•SUGGESTED MAP•	aqua3 OS Explorer 182 St Albans & Hatfield
•START / FINISH•	Grid reference: TL 291077
•DOG FRIENDLINESS•	Beware flying golf balls, hidden golf balls (fun to find, easy to swallow) and pony paddocks
•PARKING•	Lay-by opposite Five Horseshoes pub, beside recreation ground, Church Road, Little Berkhamsted
•PUBLIC TOILETS•	None on route

BACKGROUND TO THE WALK

The two small villages at each end of this walk, Essendon and Little Berkhamsted, are on ridges deeply divided by northward flowing streams heading into the Lea Valley. Beatrix Potter is known to have loved this area – she used to stay with her grandmother at Camfield Place, south of Essendon. Between the two villages you cross and re-cross a golf course, the Hatfield London Country Club. This is the former parkland to Bedwell Park, whose original emparking of 800 acres (324ha) was licenced in 1406 to John Norbury. A house was built around 1470 in brick for Sir John Say. It was visited in 1522 by Princess Mary Tudor, who was to become the last overtly Roman Catholic English monarch. Little of this house remains, it having been refronted and altered many times since, and particularly heavily in the 1860s when it also acquired a west tower. The park was extended and given an 18th-century flavour before, in the 20th century, it succumbed to the leisure industry and became a golf club. The streams have been made good use of for ornamenting and enhancing the different courses, being dammed in places to form ponds.

Little Berkhamsted

The most interesting houses in Little Berkhamsted lie to the east of the church, along the road towards the Bucks Alley junction. You emerge from Breach Lane beside the mid 18th-century, brick-fronted Little Berkhamsted House. This five-bay, three-storey structure has its roof concealed behind a parapet. Opposite is the Old Rectory, from earlier in the 18th-century, of two storeys, with five bays of box sash windows and a central, Tuscan pedimented doorcase. Looking left you see Stratton's Folly Tower, which was built to enable Admiral Stratton to see shipping on the Thames. The tower comprises several storeys and a battlemented top with a grander, arcaded storey half-way up. Returning to the church, it dates mainly from 1857 and 1894, although the south door looks like a reused Jacobean one. In addition, some of the east and west walls apparently remain from the church, which was rebuilt in 1647. Inside, some monuments from the older church were reset. The lychgate of

1904 leads back into the main village street, Church Road, and the part-Tudor Five Horseshoes pub (beside pleasant, weatherboarded cottages, opposite the church).

Stylish Essendon

Essendon's church is, in fact, much more interesting, although this also dates mostly from 1883, when it was rebuilt by the architect William White in an Arts and Crafts style. The west tower, though, is 15th century and has a poignant stone plaque on a buttress: 'A young man who suffered at Hertford for theft in 1785 begged a grave in this churchyard and prayed to God that his suffering might be a warning to others'. The 'suffering' referred to was, of course, being hanged.

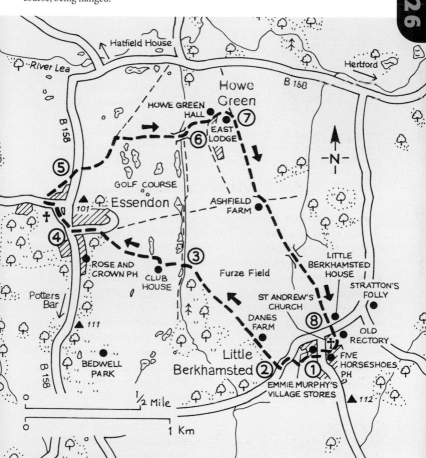

Walk 26 Directions

① From **Church Road** go through the recreation ground. At a gate turn right into a paddock. Go out through a gate and turn left, the lane descending to a bridleway sign.

② Turn right through some gates, past a white-painted estate lodge. Beyond **Danes Farm** the tarmac track becomes a green-lane bridleway. Later it descends into oak and hornbeam woodlands, bearing right and emerging past another lodge.

③ Curve left to some gates and go straight on along a metalled track, past the golf club estate's yard. Now, amid the golf course, continue towards the **club house**, a large, barn-like complex. On reaching it turn right, then left and straight on, the path now a narrow green lane. Merging with an access drive, turn left at **School Lane**.

WHAT TO LOOK FOR ⓘ

The **Old Rectory**, immediately east of St Andrew's parish church in Little Berkhamsted, is a mellow, brick, Georgian house. Here, in 1912, Brian Johnston – or 'Johnners', the well-loved cricket commentator and broadcaster, always full of gentle fun and jokes – was born. He was one of four children of Charles Johnston, who drowned tragically when Brian was only ten. Brian Johnston died in 1994.

④ Now in **Essendon**, turn right at the main road and head to the left of the war memorial to the churchyard, entering through the 1919 war memorial lychgate. Leave the churchyard near the 15th-century tower, turning left on to a lane to descend to a footpath signed 'Lower Hertford Road'. Go right, over the stile, alongside the garden of the former **Wheatsheaf** pub. Next, head across the paddock towards the left-hand house.

WHILE YOU'RE THERE ⓘ

Some 3 miles (4.8km) west of Essendon is **Hatfield House**, which is open to the public. (Unfortunately there are no public footpaths through its grounds.) In 1607 James I compelled Robert Cecil, Earl of Salisbury, to exchange Hatfield House for Theobalds (► Walk 28). Cecil built the present mansion between then and about 1612, keeping a wing of the Old Palace, built about 1480 for the Bishop of Ely, and converting it into stables.

WHERE TO EAT AND DRINK ⓘ

In Little Berkhamsted the **Five Horseshoes** serves food. Partly Tudor, it was refronted and altered around 1780. It was also once known as the Three Horseshoes! Also in Little Berkhamsted, for snacks such as biscuits, chocolate, pies and soft drinks, there is **Emmie Murphy's Village Stores** in Church Road. At Essendon there is the **Rose and Crown**.

⑤ Go over a stile, cross the road to a footpath sign. Go through a kissing gate to follow the field path parallel to the left fence. Through a gap in the hedge, re-emerge on the golf course. Cross a fairway and go straight on. Cross another fairway and descend, the metalled path becoming a grass path.

⑥ Cross the stream on a footbridge, turning left on to an access road. After about 100 paces turn right to a stile behind a horse field-shelter. Ascend the paddock, heading for a large oak tree. Over a stile turn left on to a lane, which curves right past **Howe Green Hall**.

⑦ Turn sharp right immediately past **East Lodge**. Over another stile, walk alongside the hedge, then cross a footbridge. Carry straight on across a pasture, aiming for a thick hedge. Cross the stile and go on to a bridleway to the left of **Ashfield Farm**. Cross a stream on a footbridge and head diagonally left up a long pasture field. At the top go through a gate on to a lane into **Little Berkhamsted**. To the left are views of Stratton's Folly tower.

⑧ At the road cross to the churchyard path, to the right of the **Old Rectory**. Pass the church and go through the 1909 lychgate, back into **Church Road**.

Great Wells at Great Amwell

From Hertford Heath to Great Amwell and the New River.

•DISTANCE•	6½ miles (10.4km)
•MINIMUM TIME•	2hrs 30min
•ASCENT / GRADIENT•	200ft (61m) ▲▲ ▲ ▲
•LEVEL OF DIFFICULTY•	林林 林林 林
•PATHS•	Bridleways, field paths and canal tow path, 4 stiles
•LANDSCAPE•	Well-wooded deeply cut ridge and wide valley of River Lea
•SUGGESTED MAP•	aqua3 OS Explorer 174 Epping Forest & Lee Valley
•START / FINISH•	Grid reference: TL 350116
•DOG FRIENDLINESS•	Some horse paddocks and bull warning notices
•PARKING•	Green at Church Hill or Mount Pleasant Road, Hertford Heath, off B1197
•PUBLIC TOILETS•	None on route

BACKGROUND TO THE WALK

Perched on the edge of the river cliff above the Lea Valley, is the small and most attractive village of Great Amwell. It has a pub, the George IV, and a Norman church nestled in a steeply sloping, leafy churchyard. Here are some good monuments and mausolea, including the Mylne family's, crowned by an urn.

'Amwell! Perpetual Be Thy Stream'
Below the church hill is a most attractive small lake with an island, on which stand weeping willows and an urn on a pedestal, commemorating Sir Hugh Myddelton. He constructed the New River between 1609 and 1613. Its purpose was – and still is – to carry fresh drinking water to Stoke Newington and on to London. The memorial was designed by Robert Mylne, the architect to the New River Company from 1767 until 1800. The inscription on the memorial reads: 'From the Spring at Chadwell 2 miles west and from the source of Amwell the Aqueduct meanders … conveying health, pleasure and convenience to the metropolis of Great Britain…'. On another island Mylne erected a second monument inscribed 'AMWELL! Perpetual be thy Stream Nor e'er thy spring be less…' Mylne was buried in the nearby churchyard in 1811.

Unfortunately, soon afterwards the stream failed in dry weather and the New River had to be extended northwards to the Lea between Hertford and Ware. Here the New Gauge, rebuilt in 1856, controls how much water enters the New River, the rate being 22.4 million gallons (102 million litres) a day. Remarkably, the New River is still an important element in London's water supply. (► Walks 23, 24 and 28.)

Further west, away from the Lea Valley and at the south end of the well-wooded Hertford Heath, is Haileybury College. It was opened in 1809 as a training school for the East India Company. Its architect was the Greek Revivalist William Wilkins, who also designed the National Gallery and University College London. The principal front is stone with three temple front porticos, but the walk passes along the rear where Wilkins' buildings are mostly in yellow brick. The whole is dominated, not to say overwhelmed, by Sir Arthur Blomfield's giant dome, added in 1876 (by which time Haileybury was a public school). The west arm of the walk follows a stretch of Ermine Street that is merely a track. Sections of its 'agger' are still clearly visible, and prehaps more evocative of the original Roman Road than those stretches that remain as main roads today. Named 'Ermine Street' in Anglo-Saxon times, it ran initially from London to Lincoln as a military road, probably by AD 47, within four years of the Roman Conquest. It extended to York around AD 70.

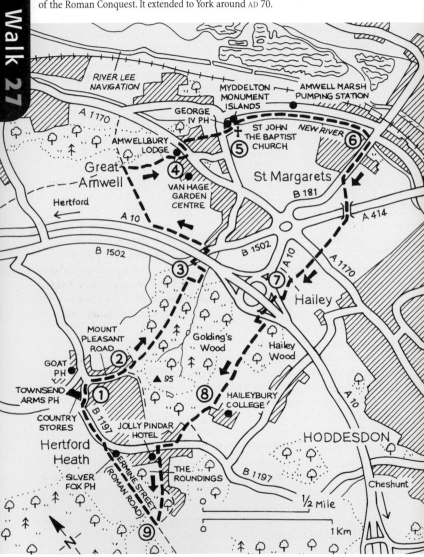

Walk 27 Directions

① Walk east along **Mount Pleasant Road** and by the Mount Pleasant sign take the left fork along a metalled track.

② At the end the bridleway bears right on to the wooded heath, then left at a bridleway post. Descend through hornbeam and oak woods, marked by occasional waymarker posts. As it becomes a sunken lane, bear right out of the wood, then

Walk 27

WHERE TO EAT AND DRINK ⓘ

In Hertford Heath are the **Silver Fox**, the **Townsend Arms** and the **Country Stores**, selling take-away soup, tea and coffee. On Church Hill's green the **Goat** is a popular choice with classic car enthusiasts. In Great Amwell try the **George IV**.

left. Cross an access lane and descend alongside the embankment of the **A10** .

③ Go under the A10, turning immediately left up to a stile, signposted 'Ware Road'. Continue alongside the A10 to a high, chain-link gate. Go through this to ascend alongside a conifer belt and reach a metalled lane at the crest.

④ Turn right. At the next road, with the **Van Hage Garden Centre** on your right, turn left by the Gothic-windowed **Amwellbury Lodge**. Shortly turn right into **Church Path** and follow the footpath to **Great Amwell**.

WHILE YOU'RE THERE ⓘ

East of the New River is another artificial watercourse, the **River Lee Navigation**. Authorised by Act of Parliament in 1739, it gave Hertfordshire's huge malt and corn trade direct access to London. The great engineers, John Smeaton and Thomas Telford, were commissioned to provide improvements, including a continuous tow path in the 1760s.

⑤ Pass the **George IV** pub and turn right into the churchyard, with its fine monuments. From the churchyard descend some steps, cross a lane and descend further, to the **New River** – the Myddelton Monument urn island is to your left. Turn right to follow the New River footpath, shortly passing **Amwell Marsh Pumping Station**.

⑥ Leave the New River at the road, turning right, uphill. Past **Hillside Lane** go left to the 'Road Used as a Public Path' sign. The track runs between fields, over the **A414**, and continues to the **A1170**. Cross this and go over a stile into pasture. Climb to the crest, go over one stile then another and turn right to descend to the **A10** roundabout.

⑦ Turn left under the A10, cross to the footpath sign and go left up the bank. At the top turn right to walk alongside woods, now in the grounds of **Haileybury College**. Continue straight on past the end of the woods on a track.

⑧ At a crossroads continue straight on along the tarmac drive, with Haileybury College on your left. The college road merges with the **B1197**. Turn left at the **Jolly Pindar Hotel**, soon with the scrubby heathland of **The Roundings** on the right. Where the road bears left, fork right on to the heath, through trees, to bear left into a wide greensward. Follow this to the road and turn right on to a track.

⑨ Now on the Roman **Ermine Street**, you follow it northwards to merge with the **B1197** through **Hertford Heath**. At the **Country Stores** shop turn right into **Church Hill** and back to the green.

WHAT TO LOOK FOR ⓘ

On the New River, south of Great Amwell, you pass **Amwell Marsh Pumping Station**. This rather fine, Italianate building of 1884 is built in yellow and red brick with stone dressings. Its function is to pump water from a well 392ft (120m) deep at the amazing rate of 3.5 million gallons (15.9 million litres) per day to supplement the New River.

Changes Around Cheshunt

From the centre of Cheshunt, taking in construction, demolition and removal.

•DISTANCE•	6 miles (9.7km)
•MINIMUM TIME•	2hrs 45min
•ASCENT / GRADIENT•	130ft (40m)
•LEVEL OF DIFFICULTY•	
•PATHS•	Lanes, footpaths, field and river paths, 7 stiles
•LANDSCAPE•	Gentle hills descending to wide valley of River Lea
•SUGGESTED MAP•	aqua3 OS Explorer 174 Epping Forest & Lee Valley
•START / FINISH•	Grid reference: TL 349023
•DOG FRIENDLINESS•	Lots of horses
•PARKING•	Churchgate, Cheshunt, east of church near Green Dragon
•PUBLIC TOILETS•	None on Walk 28; Forty Hall on Walk 29

BACKGROUND TO THE WALK

A mid the continuously built-up west side of the Lea Valley as it runs north from London to Hoddesdon, the village centre of Cheshunt, bypassed to east and west, is something of an oasis. Its parish church of St Mary was entirely rebuilt by Nicholas Dixon, the rector between 1418 and 1448. Although heavily restored since, it is a good example of a closely dated medieval building. North west of the church is a scrub- and tree-filled moated site north of (seen from the path north and from Dark Lane). Here stood the Great House, shamefully demolished in 1965. It was a mid 15th-century hall and cross wing house that had been enlarged and extended, although the original hall remained open to the roof throughout all subsequent changes. South of the church, along Churchgate, definitely the best street in the village, are the offices of Broxbourne Borough Council, modern at the south but architecturally fascinating to the north. They started life as Cheshunt College, founded by Selina, Countess of Huntingdon and moved here in 1792. The Countess of Huntingdon's Connection was an independent, nonconformist sect with its own chapels. The Georgian buildings date from this period, while the flamboyant Victorian Gothic work, complete with an incredibly ornate tower, was added in 1870. In 1905 it became a Church of England theological college before being purchased by the Council in 1970.

South east of Cheshunt village Lord Burghley built his great palace of Theobalds. It was started in 1564 and not finished until 1585. Lord Burghley spent the then colossal sum of £25,000 on the palace and grounds, with the latter including obelisks, pyramids, temples, fountains and a labyrinth. Exchanged for Hatfield House by James I in 1607, the great palace was utterly demolished in 1651 by Parliamentarian soldiers. Fragments of garden walls and of the park boundary wall – once 10 miles (16.1km) long – survive, as do bits of brickwork in a later house. This is east of the route and the Theobalds College which you do pass was Theobalds Park, a house dating from 1768, dramatically and unattractively altered and extended in Victorian and Edwardian times.

An unusual feature towards the end of the walk is Temple Bar, usually attributed to Sir Christopher Wren. It was once a gateway to the City of London, first erected in 1672 at the end of Fleet Street. When it became surplus to Victorian requirements it was re-erected here in 1889, as the north gateway to Theobalds Park.

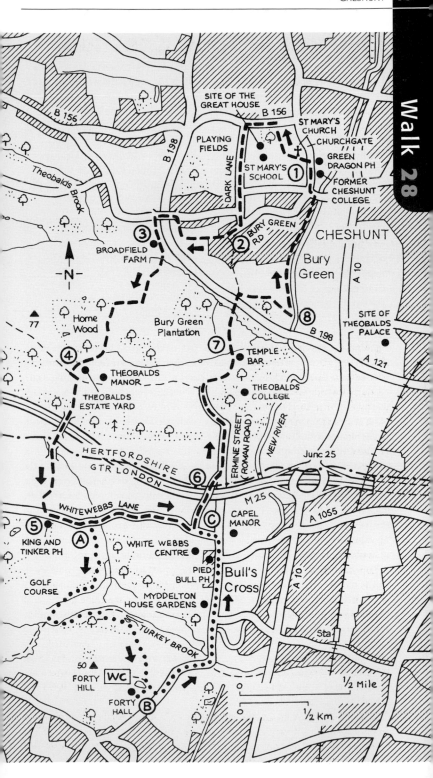

Walk 28

Walk 28 Directions

① From **Churchgate** cross the churchyard and leave by its far corner. Pass to the right of **St Mary's School**, on a path initially between fences, then playing fields. At the road go left, then left again into **Dark Lane**. Beyond **Cromwell Avenue**, pass between cemeteries into **Bury Green Road**.

② Just past No 104 turn right, on to a footpath. Go along a cul-de-sac and turn left at a T-junction, almost immediately turning right, the footpath signed 'Barrow Lane'. At the bypass the path goes right, to the road bridge.

③ Over the bridge turn left by a footpath sign, 'Whitewebbs,' along **Broadfield Farm**'s access road. Turn left at the farmyard gate, skirt some farm buildings and descend to cross **Theobalds Brook**. Now ascend the right side of a paddock. Once over a stile go right, along the edge of fields towards woods. Skirt these, left then right, to join a track by the **Theobalds Estate Yard** and turn left to a lane.

④ Turn left and, just before **Theobalds Manor**, go right, signposted 'Whitewebbs Road'. At some woods the path goes along their left side and crosses the **M25**. Descending to a stile and footbridge, follow a line of oaks to

climb another stile into pasture. At its corner go right over a bridge, the path then skirting stables towards the **King and Tinker** pub.

⑤ Turn left along **Whitewebbs Lane** (Walk 29 diverges where the parallel bridleway turns right, Point Ⓐ) and turn left opposite **White Webbs Centre** on to **Bulls Cross Ride**, signposted 'Theobalds College' (Walk 29, Point Ⓒ).

WHERE TO EAT AND DRINK
A favourite pub in this area is the **King and Tinker** on Whitewebbs Lane, full of atmosphere and small bars with good beer and food. Back in Cheshunt, you might enjoy the **Green Dragon**, a former coaching inn.

---

⑥ Across the M25 follow the lane past the **Western Cemetery**, bearing left at the gates to **Theobalds**. At a T-junction go right, on to a bridleway, initially alongside the walls of Theobalds' kitchen gardens, then along a green lane curving left.

⑦ Past **Temple Bar**, continue to the Cheshunt bypass. Across it, go right over a stile into an wood. Continue into paddocks, then through a gate by the bridge over the **New River**.

⑧ Turn left along the tow path. Walk past housing estates and leave the New River at the road bridge. Turn left and then right into **Churchgate**, passing the borough offices to the church.

WHAT TO LOOK FOR
Temple Bar, shrouded in long term scaffolding, is reputedly by the great Sir Christopher Wren, architect of St Paul's Cathedral and, from 1669, Surveyor of the King's Works. Erected in 1672, it replaced a 14th-century one seriously damaged in the 1666 Fire of London.

WHILE YOU'RE THERE
Visit the fascinating **Capel Manor College and Gardens**, Greater London's specialist horticultural and gardening college. Here are several themed gardens, the National Gardening Centre and an animal area which includes working Clydesdale horses.

A Haberdasher's Palace

Extend Walk 28 with a circuit to Sir Nicholas Raynton's Forty Hall.
See map and information panel for Walk 28

•DISTANCE•	8 miles (12.9km)
•MINIMUM TIME•	3hrs 30min
•ASCENT / GRADIENT•	215ft (66m)
•LEVEL OF DIFFICULTY•	

Walk 29 Directions
(Walk 28 option)

From Point Ⓐ turn right along the bridleway between fences, with a golf course on the right. The track bears right past and through woods, then alongside an abandoned stretch of the **New River**, now a silted stream.

Turn left to cross the New River. Just before crossing **Turkey Brook**, go left through barriers on to a grassy path, with the stream on your right. Cross a stile then turn right over a bridge and then left, signed 'Forty Hall', to follow the path, now in woods, with the stream on your left.

Continue alongside the stream before going right, across a footbridge, to a path, turning left on to a track. On the left are glimpses of small lakes before the path bears right to emerge from the woods into Forty Hall's parkland. Continue to a junction and go diagonally left, the many chimneystacks of **Forty Hall** now visible ahead. At a lime avenue turn right to a kissing gate. Skirt the lake to Forty Hall, Point Ⓑ. There are public toilets here but its museum is only open on Saturday and Sunday afternoons.

Set in parkland, Forty Hall is an early example of the red brick and hipped-roof style that continued into the Georgian period. Its builder was Sir Nicholas Raynton, a prominent London haberdasher and Lord Mayor in 1632. It belongs to a group of advanced houses built by leading citizens and those close to King Charles I's court. They abandoned the Jacobean style, exemplified by Hatfield House, in favour of a more Italian Renaissance style. Its elegant proportions and classical simplicity contrast with an elaborate interior, with strapwork decoration and more Jacobean designs.

From the house walk past the lake and follow the drive out of the park, turning left to descend Forty Hill. At the foot of the hill the road bears left to follow the course of Roman **Ermine Street**. Continue along the road, passing the entrance to **Myddelton House Gardens** and the **Pied Bull** pub. Beyond the Bullsmoor Lane junction, with the walls of **Capel Manor**'s grounds on the right, the road turns left to the junction of **Whitewebbs Lane** and **Bulls Cross Ride** – Point Ⓒ, where you rejoin Walk 28.

Aldenham and the Colne

A circuit from Aldenham's village green in improbably tranquil countryside.

•DISTANCE•	6 miles (9.7km)
•MINIMUM TIME•	2hrs 30min
•ASCENT / GRADIENT•	135ft (41m) ▲ ▲ ▲
•LEVEL OF DIFFICULTY•	👫 👫 👫
•PATHS•	Bridleways, field paths, 4 stiles
•LANDSCAPE•	Ridge overlooking Lea Valley
•SUGGESTED MAP•	aqua3 OS Explorers 173 London North; 182 St Albans & Hatfield
•START / FINISH•	Grid reference: TQ 139984 (on Explorer 173)
•DOG FRIENDLINESS•	Watch out for ponies, occasional cattle and golf balls
•PARKING•	By church in Aldenham, south of village green
•PUBLIC TOILETS•	None on route

Walk 30 Directions

From Aldenham's **parish church** head along the right edge of the green, passing to the right of its crescent of cottages built in the style of Letchworth Garden City. Aldenham is on Church Lane, a loop off the busy B462. This loop also serves the Aldenham Golf and Country Club and the University of Hertfordshire's Watford Campus (based around Wall Hall, formerly Aldenham Abbey), so all is not totally peaceful. However, the walk itself is in remarkably tranquil countryside, despite the proximity of the M1, the M25 and Watford.

Pass a modern house, **The Chequers**, on to the bridleway path, for a while parallel to the access drive to the university, with the golf course on the left. Continue along the bridleway until the track bears right, then go left at a waymarker post. Follow the path within a belt of scrub and trees, crossing many golf course tracks, until you reach a

steel, one-bar gate. Turn left, on to a lane. In 20 paces turn right over a low step-through stile and descend through a copse to the valley floor. At the access road to **Wall Hall Pumping Station** go to the right of its gates, on to a bridleway. This bridleway gives views to the right to Wall Hall and the buildings of the University of Hertfordshire, beyond the golf course. On the left, across the River Lea, you get views of Munden House amid its cedar trees. Beyond the woods that hide Wall Hall, follow the bridleway, passing **River Lodge** and bearing slightly right. Continue on this bridleway, crossing a step-over stile beside a gate. Beyond some electricity pylons the bridleway bears right. The river

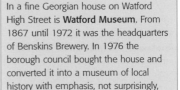

WHILE YOU'RE THERE ⓘ

In a fine Georgian house on Watford High Street is **Watford Museum**. From 1867 until 1972 it was the headquarters of Benskins Brewery. In 1976 the borough council bought the house and converted it into a museum of local history with emphasis, not surprisingly, on brewing.

also bears right and you climb to pass a pumping station, a good hedge now on the left. At a junction turn right, signposted 'Public Bridleway 72', by the entrance to **Netherwild Farm**.

The lane winds uphill to the 17th-century **Hall Farm**. Join a tarmac access road beside the farm. At a T-junction go straight over to a kissing gate. Follow the hedge in a paddock. This is very much horse country, with livery stables at the farm. Over a stile and through a gate go right on to a metalled lane. Stay on this as it ascends to the ridge then descends to pass **Blackbird Sewage Treatment Works**, joining a tarmac lane.

> ### WHERE TO EAT AND DRINK   ⓘ
> Refreshment is somewhat limited as the last pub in Aldenham village itself, the Old Red Lion, closed in 1959. However, near the end of the walk and just a little off-route is the **Round Bush** pub, which has a family garden and serves food.

Immediately past the main entrance gates go right, on to a bridleway. The path bears left, away from the sewage works, and becomes a metalled lane beyond a modern hay barn. Descend through the farmyard of **Blackbirds Farm** (which has 17th-century timber-framing), then go past some white gates and alongside some weatherboarded barns. Carry straight on, descending to the valley floor to turn left, going to the right

of the hedge and through a kissing gate. Walk along the grassy margin of an arable field, beside the hedge. Climb the hill, go through another kissing gate, and continue on the grass margin. Past a hedge-gap continue to the angle of the next field. Turn left here, over a stile to cross pasture to another stile with, away on the left, **Edge Grove House**, a late 18th-century, brick mansion that is now a preparatory school. Cross a sports field to a gate in the fence to the right of the school gates. Turn right along the main road's pavement. Cross **Church Lane** to a footpath sign.

Aldenham parish church is worth looking at for its excellent monuments, as well as its unusually wide north aisle and off-centre chancel. Interesting monuments include two medieval effigies of ladies on tomb chests in the 13th-century Lady Chapel. They are the wife and daughter-in-law of Sir William Crowmer, twice Lord Mayor of London and knighted in 1416. Perhaps the best monument (found in the north east chapel) is of John Coghill and his wife who both died in 1714. They are reclining on a tomb chest, looking remarkably casual and life-like, apparently in conversation, she raised on one elbow.

Follow the path, soon passing the 18th-century **Old Rectory** on the right. The path leads back into the churchyard and the start.

> ### WHAT TO LOOK FOR   ⓘ
> **Wall Hall** is now the University of Hertfordshire's Watford Campus; a late 18th-century farmhouse once stood on the site. George Woodford Thallason enlarged the house and took landscaping advice from the great Humphrey Repton in 1803. He then 'went Gothic'. By 1812 he had draped the house in a plethora of battlements, turrets and arched windows. To complete the fashionable and romantic medieval image he renamed the house 'Aldenham Abbey'.

Wheathampstead, Where Julius Caesar Marched

A walk from Wheathampstead along the Lea, through Devil's Dyke to Nomansland Common and back.

•DISTANCE•	5 miles (8km)
•MINIMUM TIME•	2hrs
•ASCENT / GRADIENT•	155ft (47m) ▲ ▲ ▲
•LEVEL OF DIFFICULTY•	🚶 🚶 🚶
•PATHS•	Field paths, bridleway tracks and lanes, 1 stile
•LANDSCAPE•	Valley of River Lea and gentle chalk hills
•SUGGESTED MAP•	aqua3 OS Explorer 182 St Albans & Hatfield
•START / FINISH•	Grid reference: TL 178141
•DOG FRIENDLINESS•	On leads in sheep pasture and horse paddocks on second half of walk
•PARKING•	East Lane car park, Wheathampstead
•PUBLIC TOILETS•	At car park; also by Wheathampstead Cricket Club at Nomansland (open Easter to end of September)

BACKGROUND TO THE WALK

Wheathampstead, in the Lea Valley, grew up in Anglo-Saxon times within the triangle formed by three former Roman roads. A great estate of over 12,000 acres (4,860ha), which included the site of present day Harpenden, was granted by Edward the Confessor to his Westminster Abbey in 1060.

Long before this the Wheathampstead area had been significant because the Catuvellauni – a Belgic tribe, invading from modern Belgium and northern France in the 1st century BC – made their capital here. It was a ramparted and ditched enclosure that overlooked the Lea Valley. Immediately to the east of present-day Wheathampstead and enclosing over 100 acres (40ha), the western and eastern defences of the Catuvellauni's structure survive. The eastern one is known as The Slad and the western one as the Devil's Dyke, a common Anglo-Saxon attribution for mysterious earthworks. This is probably the *oppidum* or town held by Cassivellaunus, King of the Catuvellauni, and besieged and captured in 54 BC by Julius Caesar. Our route follows the bottom of the Devil's Dyke ditch. It is 1,400ft (427m) long, 100ft (30m) across from edge to edge, and, in places, still over 40ft (12m) deep. The Slad, 600yds (549m) to the east, survives at an equally impressive scale.

Great Scott

Wheathampstead village centre is dominated by its cruciform parish church, set in a generous churchyard. The distinctive, lead-clad spire is from 1865 when the rest of the church was also restored. The transepts have very fine Decorated Gothic tracery from the 1340s which reflects the church's wealthy patronage. The north transept became the Lamer Chapel, containing memorials to the occupants of Lamer House to the north of Wheathampstead. Many are to the Garrard family, who rebuilt the house in the early 17th century. The most interesting is a bronze statuette of Apsley George Benet Cherry Garrard, in Antarctic explorer costume. He was the last of the Garrards of Lamer House and achieved fame writing *The Worst Journey in the World*, an account of Robert Falcon Scott's heroic but incompetent expedition to the South Pole from 1910 to 1913. Garrard was one of the survivors and his book, a classic tale of privation and ill-luck, is still widely read. Nomansland is not an Antarctic wasteland but a large common south of Wheathampstead. It is reputedly so called because of the bitter medieval rivalry of the abbots of Westminster (who controlled Wheathampstead) and the abbots of St Albans (who controlled Sandridge manor to the south) – the parish boundary bisects the common. The Wicked Lady pub commemorates Katherine Ferrers, the 17th-century, aristocratic highwaywoman from Markyate Cell who also terrorised travellers hereabouts (➤ Walk 41).

Walk 31

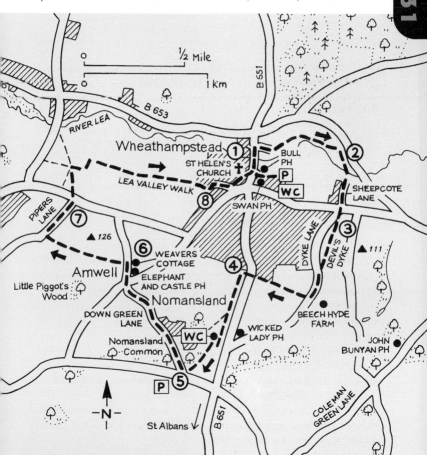

Walk 31 Directions

① Turn right past the **Bull**, go over the **River Lea** bridge and then turn right into **Mount Road**. At a bridleway sign follow the track, waymarked '**Lea Valley Walk**'. You will emerge in open countryside to wind alongside the river.

② Go through a gate with the bypass embankment ahead of you, and turn right. Go between some fences and through another gate, then bear right on to a metalled track, re-crossing the Lea. Now on **Sheepcote Lane**, go uphill, over the main road into **Dyke Lane**.

③ By **Tudor Road** go left on to a footpath along the remarkably deep ditch of **Devil's Dyke**. Emerging at a lane, turn left and follow it, then go right at a footpath sign opposite **Beech Hyde Farm**. Now on a grass track amid arable fields, pass modern housing to the right, to reach a road.

WHAT TO LOOK FOR ⓘ

In **St Helen's Church**, Wheathampstead, are several fittings from the private chapel of the Garrard family of Lamers a mile (1.6km) north of the village, the odd name a corruption of de la Mare. The mansion was built in 1632 and the fittings come from this house, demolished in 1761. They include the hexagonal pulpit, dated 1634, the communion table and benches in the north transept, one dated 1641.

---

④ Cross the road to a footpath signposted 'Nomansland', and turn left on to a tarmac track – the road runs parallel, to your left. Walk downhill to the **Wicked Lady** pub and turn right on to the access drive to **Wheathampstead Cricket Club**. Pass behind the pavilion to a footpath. Turn left past some cricket nets, the path winding through trees. Across a clearing, ignore a path to the right and continue through the trees to another clearing. Head towards a bench in an oak copse, then to another bench where the path bears right to the road.

⑤ At **Nomansland car park** you turn right into **Down Green Lane**, which leads off the common. At a crossroads carry straight on, past the **Elephant and Castle** pub.

WHILE YOU'RE THERE ⓘ

Just a mile (1.6km) south east of Wheathampstead, at Coleman Green, is the **John Bunyan** pub (formerly the Prince of Wales). It commemorates the Puritan preacher, John Bunyan, a Bedfordshire man, famed for his book, *The Pilgrim's Progress*, published in 1678. He stayed in a house near by, now gone. **Coleman Green Lane** is a good stretch of the former Roman road from St Albans to Welwyn, which became a medieval lane.

---

⑥ Shortly, opposite **Weavers Cottage**, go left at a footpath sign and up a few steps. The path passes a golf course, then crosses some cultivated land to reach a road, **Pipers Lane**. Turn right.

⑦ At a T-junction go straight across and over a stile, heading diagonally left across pasture to a stile and right on to a track. Turn immediately right on to a muddy track which shortly turns left downhill between horse fences, then right over a stile. After about a mile (1.6km) housing appears on the left, the path becomes tarmac and jinks to a road.

⑧ Go left into **High Meads** and then right to descend into **Wheathampstead**. At **Bury Green** go left to the church. From the churchyard go left into the **High Street** and the end of the walk.

WHERE TO EAT AND DRINK ⓘ

The **Bull**, by the car park at the start of the walk in Wheathampstead, serves food. It has 17th-century, timber-framing, and has been a pub since at least 1617. The **Swan** in the High Street is older, partly about 1500 and partly 17th-century. At Nomansland the **Wicked Lady** has 'family dining' and a garden with outdoor play equipment.

Athenian Influence at Ayot House and Shaw Corner

A walk from Ayot St Lawrence to Ayot St Peter and back, via the last home of George Bernard Shaw.

•DISTANCE•	5 miles (8km)
•MINIMUM TIME•	2hrs
•ASCENT / GRADIENT•	120ft (37m)
•LEVEL OF DIFFICULTY•	🚶🚶 🚶 🚶
•PATHS•	Bridleways, former railway line and field paths, 2 stiles
•LANDSCAPE•	Gently rolling arable countryside with woodland stretches
•SUGGESTED MAP•	aqua3 OS Explorer 182 St Albans & Hatfield
•START / FINISH•	Grid reference: TL 195168
•DOG FRIENDLINESS•	On lead through pasture around Ayot St Lawrence with horses and sheep
•PARKING•	Roadside parking in Ayot St Lawrence near Brocket Arms
•PUBLIC TOILETS•	None on route

BACKGROUND TO THE WALK

Ayot St Lawrence is only accessible by winding country lanes, and yet it is immensely popular with visitors and walkers. Notwithstanding the two churches and the Brocket Arms pub, the main draw is Shaw Corner. This Edwardian villa, built as a rectory, was George Bernard Shaw's home from 1906 until his death in 1950.

Sir Lionel Lyde

In the village stands the ruined old church of St Lawrence. Sir Lionel Lyde, the lord of the manor, decided to rebuild the church in a different location and set his men to pull the church down, apparently without informing the Bishop of Lincoln, in whose diocese it stood. The bishop ordered the work to stop; Lyde obeyed, but made no effort to make good the damage. Instead he just continued with his project, the remarkable Greek-style new church which he wanted as an eye-catcher for his mansion, Ayot House. You can see the effect by standing in Lyde's sheep-cropped park with its oaks, pines and sycamores. Look across to the early 18th century, three-storey brick façade of Ayot House with its parapet and box sash windows. Sir Lionel Lyde was a tobacco merchant and a director of the Bank of England and he, of course, looked west to the new church, built in what was then a very advanced style of architecture. He used the architect Nicholas Revett, who with James 'Athenian' Stuart had published *Antiquities of Athens*, the first volume arriving in 1762. Revett designed a Greek temple with side colonnades linking it to pedimented pavilions. The main portico copied that of the Temple of Apollo at Delos and, designed in 1778, it was consecrated in July 1779.

Til Death Us Do Part

At one end pavilion is an urn under which Sir Lionel is buried and at the other end pavilion, under another urn, his wife is buried. Apparently their marriage was unhappy and the knight took the view that the church, having united them in holy matrimony, should physically keep them apart in death. Certainly it is a remarkable design for the 1770s and a telling demonstration of the dictatorial powers of Georgian land-owning gentry. Ayot St Peter's parish church is a complete contrast. A muscular Victorian church in red and blue brick with stone dressings, Earl Cowper laid its foundation stone in April 1875. It was the fourth church to be built in the parish. The first three were in the present cemetery north of the tiny village (by Tamarisk Cottage) where the lane goes sharply left. The third church, built in 1751, was octagonal with a separate bell tower. Although it mostly burnt down in 1874, its chancel survived and it now serves as a mortuary chapel.

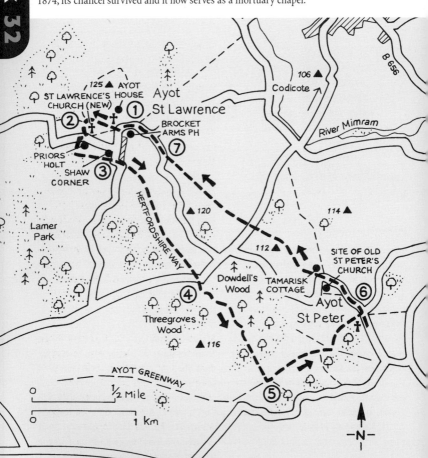

Walk 32 Directions

① From the roadside near the **Brocket Arms**, head west past the ruined medieval **Church of St Lawrence** and, at the bend, go to the right of a telephone box through a kissing gate. The portico

of the old church should be straight ahead of you. Now in pasture, take the right-hand fork path, with a post-and-wire fence to your right. Go through another kissing gate and cross pasture grazed by sheep to St Lawrence's 'new' church, entering the churchyard via a third kissing gate.

Walk 32

② Leave the churchyard from behind the church, along a metalled access drive. At the lane go right, signposted 'Hertfordshire Way', then go left past **Priors Holt** at a stile and footpath sign into pasture. At another stile descend some steps to a path along the edge of a wood. Turn left to follow it, passing the leafy grounds of **Shaw Corner**, to reach a road.

WHAT TO LOOK FOR ⓘ
Before Ayot St Peter you walk along part of the old **Hertford, Luton and Dunstable Railway**, opened in 1858 and closed in 1965. It was called 'the Hatters Line' because much of its freight traffic was straw hats made in and around Luton, the centre of the straw-plaiting industry. Today the trackbed serves as a footpath between Welwyn Garden City and Wheathampstead.

③ Turn right and in a short while, where the road swings to the right, go straight on at the public bridleway sign. Follow the bridleway, which is a narrow, high-hedged and often muddy green lane for much of its length. At the summit a bypass footpath through scrub avoids the muddiest sections of the bridleway. Go through a wooded kissing gate and follow the path as it winds amid a belt of beautiful oak and hornbeam trees to a road via a kissing gate.

WHILE YOU'RE THERE ⓘ
Shaw Corner was presented to the National Trust by George Bernard Shaw (1856–1950) in his lifetime and he died here after falling from an apple tree he was pruning at the ripe old age of 94. His country home from 1906, it is preserved much as he left it and his writing summerhouse survives. Here he worked on many of his most well-known plays such as *Pygmalion* and *Saint Joan*.

WHERE TO EAT AND DRINK ⓘ
The **Brocket Arms** in Ayot St Lawrence is an immensely popular pub with good food and has been a pub since at least 1694, although called the Three Horseshoes until 1937. Part timber-framed with a mellow old tile roof concealing in part a 15th-century king post roof, it has 18th-century alterations and additions.

④ At the road, jink left then right to a public bridleway sign. Walk alongside oak and hornbeam coppiced woodland. Through a conifer copse the path emerges, now in an arable field, with a hedge to your left. Ahead of you is the embankment of the old **Hatters Line railway**.

⑤ Go right at the railway bridge to climb the embankment and then left, back across the bridge. Follow the old trackbed until just before the start of some woods. Here go left over a stile. Bear right, ignoring the left hand path, and skirt the woods, later entering them on an old holloway track.

⑥ At the road go right to visit **Ayot St Peter church**. Retrace your steps past the former school and continue along the lane until it turns sharp left at a cemetery. You go straight on to a grassy track to the left of **Tamarisk Cottage**. Follow the bridleway, much of it a hedgeless track between arable fields, cross a road and continue on the bridleway.

⑦ Pass through a hedge to a lane opposite **Stocking Lane Cottage** and turn right uphill to a road junction. At **Lord Mead Lane** go left, signposted 'Shaw Corner' and bear left back to the **Brocket Arms** pub and the start.

Ebenezer's Welwyn Vision

From the centre of ground-breaking Welwyn Garden City to Brocket Park,
Sherrardspark Wood and the Hatters Line railway path.

•DISTANCE•	4 miles (6.4km)
•MINIMUM TIME•	2hrs
•ASCENT / GRADIENT•	120ft (37m) ▲▲ ▲▲▲
•LEVEL OF DIFFICULTY•	🚶🚶 🚶🚶 🚶🚶
•PATHS•	Town roads, parkland paths and woodland tracks, 3 stiles
•LANDSCAPE•	Garden City, 18th-century parkland (and golf course) and mixed woodland
•SUGGESTED MAP•	aqua3 OS Explorer 182 St Albans & Hatfield
•START / FINISH•	Grid reference: TL 235133
•DOG FRIENDLINESS•	On leads on town roads and golf course
•PARKING•	Campus West Long Term car park (free on Sundays) off B195 in Welwyn Garden City
•PUBLIC TOILETS•	East of John Lewis in Wigmores, Welwyn Garden City

BACKGROUND TO THE WALK

Hertfordshire has a key place in the history of the Garden City Movement. Within the county are Letchworth, started in 1903, and Welwyn Garden City, the theme of this walk, started in 1920. The movement was the inspiration of the utopian socialist Ebenezer Howard, who published the cumbersomely titled *Tomorrow: A Peaceful Path to Real Reform* in 1898. It inspired the foundation of the Garden City Association in 1899 and the book was rewritten in 1902 with the somewhat snappier title, *Garden Cities of Tomorrow*.

Complete Town

Letchworth was started by Howard in nearly 4,000 acres (1,620ha) of land to the west of Baldock. After the First World War he began his next venture, refining his ideas after the lessons of Letchworth. Howard bought 1,688 acres (684ha) south east of Welwyn at auction from the Cowper estate in May 1919, adding a further 694 acres (281ha) in October of that year. In April 1920 he formed Welwyn Garden City Limited and the first houses were occupied by Christmas. The aim of both Letchworth and Welwyn Garden City was to create a complete town with industry and commerce giving a viable economic base. The railway that cuts through the middle of the city, running north to south, had a profound influence on its layout, which was master-minded by a young, idealistic architect called Louis de Soissons. The principal boulevard is Parkway, which has parallel avenues of trees. Parkway and the semi-circular Campus at its north end have the same axis as the railway, which also served to separate the city into two. On the east side were working class housing and factories. West of Parkway is middle class housing, much of it occupied by commuters to London. Our route crosses The Campus, goes down Parkway and then west to wind through the middle class housing with its trees and hedges, many retained from the previous farmland. The style of buildings here is 'cottage Georgian', which works well at this scale. However, to the east of Parkway the larger-scale 1930s buildings, also by de Soissons, are in an over-blown Neo-Georgian style, complete with pedimented porticos or temple fronts.

Welwyn is a remarkable achievement. Its shredded wheat factory, designed by de Soissons in 1925, is now a listed building. Other notable early factories included Norton Abrasives and Roche, whose laboratories and offices, opened in 1938. After the Second World War a third generation of planned towns arrived and Hertfordshire received its fair share – Stevenage, Hemel Hempstead and Hatfield.

Walk 33

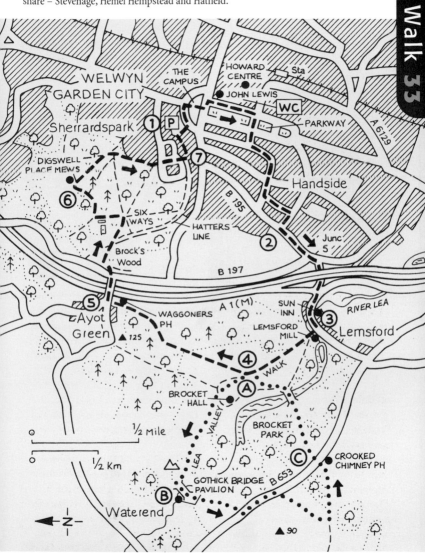

Walk 33 Directions

① Cross **The Campus**, a semi-circular, leafy open space, and pass to the right of a large department store, along **Parkway**. At the traffic lights cross right, into **Church Road**. At its end turn left into **Guessens Road**, which curves right. Cross **Handside Lane** into **Youngs Rise** and then turn left into **Elm Gardens**. At the end turn right into **Applecroft Road**.

Walk 33

② Turn left into **Valley Road**. Leaving Welwyn Garden City, go under the **A1(M)** bridge and straight on into **Lemsford** village, with the **River Lea** to your left.

③ At **Lemsford Mill** turn right to cross the river on a stylish modern bridge. Follow the footpath and bear right at a junction, now on the **Lea Valley Walk**. You are soon in **Brocket Park**, this part a golf course. Carry straight on where the right-hand fence ends. Cross a tarmac path to a footpath post (Point Ⓐ, where Walk 34 diverges) – a thatched tennis pavilion is behind the fence here.

④ Turn right but follow the drive for only about 20 paces, then carry straight on across the golf course, guided by waymarker posts. The footpath climbs right, out of a dry valley and, passing a cottage, you climb a stile out of Brocket Park. Over another stile turn left into **Brickwall Close**, with the **Waggoners** pub on the right. At **Ayot Green** turn right and cross over the **A1(M)**.

⑤ At the T-junction turn left and almost immediately right, down to a stile leading into some woods. Go diagonally left, not sharp right. When you reach a bridleway junction bear right, the path

descending to cross the course of an old railway line. At **Six Ways** (which has carved totem poles) turn sharp left on to a bridleway. Pass through a car park to a lane. Turn right, with the parkland to **Digswell Place** on your left.

⑥ At **Digswell Place Mews** turn right by a waymarker post, to return to the woods. At a bridleway post bear right uphill – the path carries on straight through the woods. Ignore all turns to the left and right until you near the gardens of houses. Turn right to walk alongside their fences, eventually bearing left to merge with a track and leave the woods. Go straight over **Reddings** into **Roundwood Drive** and on to a tarmac path between gardens.

⑦ Turn left on to the old railway trackbed (the **Hatters Line**). Turn right up a fenced ramp, out of the cutting and back into the **Campus West car park**.

Brocket Hall Reflections

Take a circuit of an 18th-century park to a Palladian mansion.
See map and information panel for Walk 33

•DISTANCE•	2 miles (3.2km)
•MINIMUM TIME•	1hr
•ASCENT / GRADIENT•	85ft (26m)
•LEVEL OF DIFFICULTY•	

Walk 34 Directions (Walk 33 option)

From Point Ⓐ walk alongside the fence. **Brocket Hall**'s private grounds are on your left, the golf course is on your right. Cross an access road via a stile, then keep along the right hand side of the fence. Follow the waymarker posts, enjoying views of Brocket Hall.

Brocket Hall's parkland was made picturesque in 'Capability' Brown style by a Mr Wood, at the same time that the house was rebuilt. The lake was created by damming the River Lea. The fine bridge was designed by James Paine. He also designed the mansion for Sir Matthew Lamb in the 1760s, replacing a late-Tudor courtyard house. The latter had been built by Sir John Brocket, whose family had held the estate since the 1470s. Paine's austere exterior hides a more sumptuous interior, including work by Robert Adam.

A later owner was William Lamb, who as Lord Melbourne, was the young Queen Victoria's avuncular guide and her first Prime Minister. William Lamb's brother-in-law was Lord Palmerston, who inherited Brocket Hall in 1848 and also later became Prime Minister (► Walk 17).

Keep straight on across the parkland, guided by waymarker posts, to enter oak and chestnut woodland. The path descends steeply to the valley floor. Here, Point Ⓑ, turn left on to a track, leaving the Lea Valley Walk.

Cross the **River Lea** where a flint-fronted, **Gothick bridge pavilion** is to your right. Now the track bears left and climbs out of the valley, still in woodland, to a road. Turn left and, passing the entrance to **Brocket Hall Golf Club** and **Auberge du Lac** restaurant, immediately cross the road to a stile. Once over the stile go diagonally left across a field to a farm access road. Turn left to the main road, Point Ⓒ, where there is a fine view of Brocket Hall beyond the beautiful wrought-iron gate.

With the **Crooked Chimney** pub on the right, cross a stile to re-enter **Brocket Park**. The path descends, with woods to your right and parkland to your left. Join the drive to cross **James Paine's bridge** over the lake. Continue, passing the gates to the private drive to **Brocket Hall**, back to Point Ⓐ.

Roman Verulamium

A walk through Roman Verulamium and the medieval town of St Albans.

•**DISTANCE**•	3¾ miles (6km)
•**MINIMUM TIME**•	2hrs 30min
•**ASCENT / GRADIENT**•	115ft (35m) ▲ ▲ ▲
•**LEVEL OF DIFFICULTY**•	👫 👫 👫
•**PATHS**•	Urban streets then parkland, no stiles
•**LANDSCAPE**•	Gentle hills, parkland, a Roman site and historic streets
•**SUGGESTED MAP**•	aqua3 OS Explorer 182 St Albans & Hatfield
•**START / FINISH**•	Grid reference: TL 141065
•**DOG FRIENDLINESS**•	On leads in St Albans but can roam free in parkland
•**PARKING**•	Car park between Abbey Theatre/Westminster Lodge Leisure Centre and Athletics Track Arena, off Holywell Hill
•**PUBLIC TOILETS**•	Fishpool Street and Town Hall

Walk 35 Directions

The walk starts in the Roman city of Verulamium, built on the west bank of the River Ver, and covers the half south of Bluehouse Hill (the A4147, which still follows the course of the Roman street from the west gate to the east).

From the car park follow the tarmac path past the **Athletics Track Arena** and at the signpost turn left, signed 'Roman Gate and Walls'. This section of path shows you the scale of the Roman town and its defences, passing first the site of the south gate, or Watling Street gate, on your right, its outlines set out in the grass. Beyond this you walk alongside the longest surviving stretch of the town's great walls, built between AD 252 and 270. These rubble walls with bands of thin Roman bricks survive from 6ft (2m) to 9ft (3m) high, but when built they rose to 23ft (7m). To your left is a spectacular stretch of Roman ditch, albeit now filled with

trees and scrub, up to 95ft (29m) across and 20ft (6.1m) deep.

At the road turn right. After less than 40 paces go right on a path down into the south west section of the Roman ditch. Emerging from the trees and scrub, head across grass towards a red, dog-waste bin and pass between two sycamores. Turn right here on to a path to the left of a residual hedge. Descend, towards the tower of **St Michael's Church**. Join a track to the right of the hedge. The site of the Roman city's forum or central square is on your left. The church was built on the site of the basilica or town hall. Ahead is the **Verulamium Museum**.

Turn left at **Ladies Gate** to the church. The church contains reused Roman tiles and is mainly Anglo-Saxon with Norman aisles. Leave the churchyard through the gate and turn left past the school. Cross the main road to the Roman theatre site. Retrace your steps to continue along **St Michael's Street**, heading for the **River Ver**, which has fine,

Walk 35

timber-framed houses on each side. Over the river, past the **Kingsbury Water Mill Museum**, go right into **Fishpool Street**, which winds uphill in the lee of the Anglo-Saxon burh, **Kingsbury**. Fishpool Street – one of the best streets in St Albans – was named after the fishponds on the River Ver. The buildings are mainly two storey and a mixture of timber-framed and jettied houses and Georgian and later brick fronts. Pass **Romeland**, the former market place at the gates of the medieval abbey. Continue into **George Street**.

Cross into **High Street** and then turn left into **French Row**. Pass the **Clock Tower**, a rare medieval curfew belfry built around 1410, and, on the left, the fleur-de-lys. In a house on this site (the present inn dates from the 1420s) King Jean of France was held prisoner after the Battle of Poitiers in 1356.

Continue along **French Row** to the market place, passing the former Corn Exchange and the imposing Town Hall of 1831 with its Ionic

columned portico. The best buildings in the long market place are the Georgian fronts on the eastern side, towards the **Hatfield Road** roundabout. Beyond is **St Peter's Church**, which dominates views in this direction.

Retrace your steps, passing to the left of the **Town Hall**, then cross the High Street junction. Go downhill and turn right, opposite the timber-framed **White Hart Hotel**, into **Sumpter Yard**. Here you can visit the former Abbey church with its great Norman crossing tower and the reconstructed shrine to St Alban, Britannia's first Christian martyr who died in AD 304. Continue alongside the nave to the gatehouse from the 1360s. This is the only substantial remnant of one of medieval England's wealthiest and most powerful abbeys.

Now turn left down **Abbey Mill Lane** and descend to the mill gates, turning right on to a path past **Ye Olde Fighting Cocks**. Turn left over the bridge. On the left is **Abbey Mills**, a medieval mill converted to a silk mill in the 18th century. Walk past the lakes, enlarged from the Abbey's medieval fish ponds or 'stews' into ornamental lakes in the 1920s. Beyond is a stretch of Roman wall. Turn left at the footpath sign to walk back, past the athletics track, to the car park.

Walk 36

Chess and Colne Meeting

A walk across Chorleywood Common to Rickmansworth.

•DISTANCE•	7½ miles (12.1km)
•MINIMUM TIME•	3hrs
•ASCENT / GRADIENT•	210ft (64m) ▲▲▲
•LEVEL OF DIFFICULTY•	🚶 🚶 🚶
•PATHS•	Field paths, footpaths, canal tow path and some town pavements, no stiles
•LANDSCAPE•	Common, river valleys and water-meadows
•SUGGESTED MAP•	aqua3 OS Explorer 172 Chiltern Hills East
•START / FINISH•	Grid reference: TQ 033966
•DOG FRIENDLINESS•	Great dog-socialising on Chorleywood Common; some pavements and horse paddocks
•PARKING•	Car park off A404 Rickmansworth Road on Chorleywood Common
•PUBLIC TOILETS•	None on route

BACKGROUND TO THE WALK

Chorleywood Common is one of several commons in West Hertfordshire that survived 19th-century attempts at enclosure. Covering over 200 acres (81ha), it is a haven for dog-walkers (and golfers). The east side of the common has a rather good church – its distinctive spire is a local landmark. The church is an 1869 rebuild by G E Street of an earlier one erected in 1845 when Chorleywood became a separate parish. Beside it is the church school, parts of which date back to 1853.

Lines of Transport

To the west is 'Metroland' Chorleywood, which grew up around the railway. The station opened in the late 1880s and this walk passes under the Metropolitan Line which runs along the south side of the common. Going back a century, as you approach Rickmansworth you follow the Grand Union Canal. It was originally called the Grand Junction Canal. In 1796 it was opened from London as far as Batchworth Lock.

On the left, between the canal and the winding course of the River Colne, is the Rickmansworth Aquadrome, in a former gravel pit which has been flooded. There are other similarly flooded pits here, such as Stocker's Lake, now forming nature reserves where you can see a wide variety of waterfowl. On the right of the canal a large Tesco's has been built on the site of Frogmoor Wharf. Here, canal boats were built and coal and building materials were traded – at least its stone name-plaque has been preserved.

Church Street

Rickmansworth has suffered from over-zealous redevelopment through its northern and western relief roads, leading to considerable architectural loss. However, Church Street retains much of its character and several older buildings of note. The early 16th-century, timber-framed Priory (north of the church) was never a priory, of course, but was probably a church house or 'marriage-feast' house. The church itself looks good but is entirely post-medieval. The tower dates from 1630 but the rest is 19th-century. Further up Church Street, the Feathers pub is partly Tudor and the vicarage has late medieval timber-framing. To the west of the church stands the town's best building, The Bury, now divided into apartments. It is Tudor and 17th century, and was the manor house until 1741. North of Rickmansworth our route along the Chess Valley gives views of an apparent Neo-Georgian town set in parkland on the hill to the west – this is the Royal Masonic School, built in the 1930s and replacing the successor manor house, Bury Park Manor House.

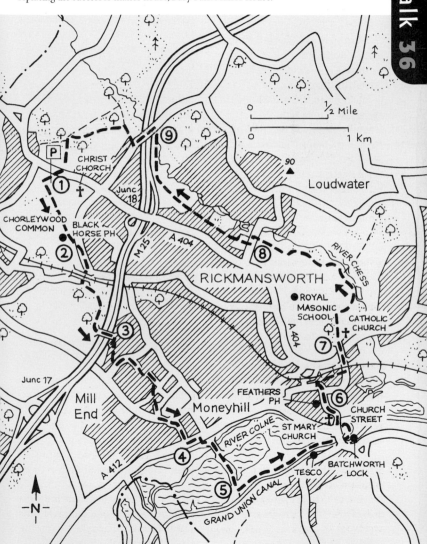

Walk 36 Directions

① From the car park head along the ride cut through the trees of

Chorleywood Common. Ignoring a cross-track, turn left at the next crossroad of rides. Keep straight on, eventually merging with a lane close to the **Black Horse** pub.

Walk 36

② Turn right. At a T-junction again turn right, into **Berry Lane**. Go, under the railway bridge then turn left on to a woodland footpath, signposted 'Mill End'. Shortly take the right fork to climb out of the valley, then alongside the **M25**, crossing it on a footbridge.

③ Turn right on to a path behind garden fences, then turn left through a barrier to a housing estate. Turn right then, at a T-junction, go left into **Chiltern Drive**. Next turn right into **Coombe Hill Road** and then go straight on along a path to a cul-de-sac. Turn right by No 13 then cross another green and a further path between gardens. At a road go right and at the T-junction go left along **Church Lane** to the main road.

④ Turn left and, past the bus stop, go right at the footpath sign. Over a footbridge turn left, then right, over the **River Colne** on a bigger bridge. Follow the footpath between large lakes (old gravel pits).

⑤ Turn left on to the **Grand Union Canal** tow path and follow this to **Rickmansworth**. Under the bypass bridge turn left up some steps to the road. Go right to the roundabout, carrying straight on into **Church Street**.

⑥ Go straight over Rickmansworth's High Street's crossroads into **Northway**, which curves left. Turn right into

WHERE TO EAT AND DRINK ⓘ
In Rickmansworth there is quite a choice for eating and drinking. The most interesting building is the **Feathers** in Church Street. Out in the country try the **Black Horse** on the edge of Chorleywood Common.

WHILE YOU'RE THERE ⓘ
Between suburban Chorleywood and Junction 17 of the M25 is **Heronsgate**. The pioneering Chartist and socialist Daniel O'Connor founded the settlement, initially named O'Connorville, in 1846. It was an idealistic attempt by his National Land Company to provide smallholdings. Like many utopian dreams it soon went bankrupt. However, many of the cottages survive, now as pricey 'Metroland' dwellings.

Solomon's Hill between blocks of flats, then right again on to a footpath alongside the railway. Turn left at the road and cross the **A412** on the footbridge.

⑦ Go to the path, waymarked 'Chess Valley Walk', to the left of the **Catholic church**, to reach the banks of the **River Chess**. Continue on the west bank to skirt a wood.

WHAT TO LOOK FOR ⓘ
At **Batchworth Lock** on the Grand Union Canal in Rickmansworth under Bridge 173 you face two canals. On the right is the Grand Union, on the left is a stretch of the River Chess that was canalised in 1804 for the long-gone Salters Brewery.

⑧ Beyond some paddocks cross a road, continuing on the **Chess Valley Walk**. Bear right at a path fork, cross another road and go through more pony paddocks to walk alongside the M25.

⑨ At the road turn left, over the **M25**, going right at a footpath sign just before some houses, still on the Chess Valley Walk. Where the tarmac track bears right go left, to the path within the edge of woods. Follow the path uphill. At a T-junction go left into a park and follow the road past the cemetery to the gates and the car park.

Walk 37

Around the Chess Valley

Walk through Flaunden, Sarratt and the water-meadows of the Chess Valley.

•DISTANCE•	7 miles (11.3km)
•MINIMUM TIME•	2hrs 45min
•ASCENT / GRADIENT•	245ft (75m) ▲▲▲
•LEVEL OF DIFFICULTY•	𝕩 𝕩 𝕩
•PATHS•	Paths, tracks, village roads and country lanes, 5 stiles
•LANDSCAPE•	Chalk plateau and water-meadows
•SUGGESTED MAP•	aqua3 OS Explorers 172 Chiltern Hills East; 182 St Albans & Hatfield
•START / FINISH•	Grid reference:TQ 042994 (on Explorer 172)
•DOG FRIENDLINESS•	Frequent horses and cattle; one bull warning sign
•PARKING•	On west side of Sarratt Green
•PUBLIC TOILETS•	None on route

BACKGROUND TO THE WALK

In the late 18th century Flaunden village migrated uphill to cottages built by Lord Latimer, who owned the manor. These rows of flint and brick cottages remain today. In 1838 the rector of Latimer's nephew, the young George Gilbert Scott, designed his first church here, a humble start for the great Victorian architect. He later described it as 'the poor barn'.

On a romantic site, within a copse in the water-meadows of the River Chess, is the lost church of Flaunden. East of Latimer village, you can leave the path to read an information board that tells the story of Flaunden's old church. Built in about 1230 for Thomas de Faundel, it was a small cruciform church, in the shape of a Greek cross with arms of equal length. Now vanished, in 1910 it was still standing but described thus: 'Condition – Very bad; the ruins are loaded with heavy ivy, and much damage has been done by visitors'. The old church was abandoned and partially dismantled when the new one opened further up the hill, reusing the old font and a few floor tiles. There is a non-churchyard burial further east of the old church, alongside the Chess Valley Walk. It is the tomb of William Liberty who died in 1777 and consists of a brick structure with a stone slab, surrounded by railings.

Watercress and Cattle

Further east along the Chess Valley, south of Valley Farm, are working watercress beds, once a common sight along the Chess and many of the Chilterns' other rivers, such as the Misbourne, Ver and Gade. Back up on the Chiltern plateau, Sarratt is a village of two distinct parts. The original centre around the church is over ¹⁄₂ mile (800m) from the present core of the village, which is clustered around the long, narrow green, itself ¹⁄₂ mile (800m) from end to end. Sarratt was a famous droving stop on cattle and sheep routes to London. At one time there were more than five pubs as well as three ponds for watering the stock. The village gravitated to the green, leaving the church in comparative isolation, with just the manor house, a couple of cottages, the Cock Inn and the row of almshouse, with Gothic-arched windows, built by Ralph Day of Sarratt Hall in 1821. Sarratt's Church of the Holy Cross is an almost complete one from around 1190. Its chancel was lengthened later in the Middle Ages and a west tower was added to the short two-bay nave.

Commonwood

½ mile

½ km

Belsize

BOOT PH

Sarratt

CRICKETERS PH

▲ 115

Croxley Green

HOLY CROSS CHURCH

(1)

POST OFFICE STORES

(8) COCK INN

ALMSHOUSES

Church End

▲ 128

GREAT SARRATT FARM

CHILTERN WAY

CAKEBREAD COTTAGE

RIVER CHESS

ROSE HALL FARM

(7)

BRAGMAN'S FARM

Hanginglane Wood

CRESS BEDS

(2)

NEWHOUSE FARM

CHESS VALLEY WALK

Chorleywood

Chenies

▲ 140

(3)

OAK COTTAGE

(6)

MILL FARM

CHENIES MANOR ▲ 125

A 404

Flaunden

ST MARY MAGDALENE CHURCH

▲ 140

Baldwin's Wood

SITE OF FLAUNDEN OLD CHURCH

(4)

LIBERTY'S TOMB

HERTFORDSHIRE

BUCKINGHAMSHIRE

Latimer

N

(5)

Walk 37 Directions

① From **Sarratt Green** walk north. Beyond **Great Sarratt Farm** go left, signed 'Rose Hall'. Bear right across pastures then go along a lane, beside some woods, now on the **Chiltern Way**. Take the left fork to skirt **Rose Hall Farm** to a path. Over a stile skirt right of the barns of **Bragman's Farm** to the lane.

② Turn left uphill and go right at a Chiltern Way sign. Head left to a stile, then by the hedge to a lane. Turn right. Past **Newhouse Farm** turn left on to a path. At a stile go diagonally right across a field and, at the hedge, bear right to a lane.

③ Turn left and walk through **Flaunden**. At the church turn left on to a bridleway. Follow this to a T-junction by two small observatories and turn right.

WHAT TO LOOK FOR   **i**

Along the Chess Valley, between Points ⑥ and ⑦, you pass working **watercress beds**, making good use of the fast flowing clean, chalk stream. Rich in dissolved lime, its waters are ideal for growing this nutritious crop.

---

④ As the lane goes left, carry on along a bridleway into woods. Go left, ignoring a path to the right. Fork right and descend steeply. Emerging from the wood descend between fences to the road.

⑤ Turn left, pass **Latimer** green, and turn left again on the **Chess Valley Walk**. Descend to an information board about Flaunden old church. Rejoin the path and, passing Liberty's tomb, follow the waymarks through **Mill Farm** and turn left on to a lane.

⑥ After about 150yds (137m) leave the lane on the right and carry on over a stile, on the **Chess Valley Walk**. Through a wood follow the path between fences. When you reach a concrete access road go straight on, with working cress beds on your right.

WHILE YOU'RE THERE   **i**

Just over the Buckinghamshire border south of the River Chess is **Chenies Manor** which is often open to the public. A Tudor brick house of the late 15th century built for the Cheynes, it passed in 1526 to the Russells, later the Dukes of Bedford. Prominent courtiers, they added a grand brick range of lodgings with massive chimney stacks.

---

⑦ At the lane turn right, turning left uphill at a T-junction, leaving the Chess Valley Walk. Beyond **Cakebread Cottage** go right, through a gate. Ascend alongside a hedge, go over a stile and cross pasture to join a sycamore and beech avenue, then walk alongside a holly hedge to Sarratt churchyard.

⑧ Retrace your steps out of the churchyard and bear diagonally right towards the woods – you will reach them at a Chiltern Way signpost. Continue along the wood edge, then cross a drive to a kissing gate. Follow the path through a copse, then alongside a hedge through cattle pasture to emerge between houses into **Sarratt Green**.

WHERE TO EAT AND DRINK   **i**

Two pubs at Sarratt Green are the **Cricketers** (by the south pond) and the **Boot** (half-way along the green). By Sarratt's church is the **Cock Inn** and in Flaunden is the **Green Dragon**. All of the pubs serve food. Also, at the start on Sarratt Green there is the **Sarratt Post Office Store and Off-licence** for snacks.

In Rothamsted Park

A walk from Harpenden and its common, through Rothamsted Park.

•DISTANCE•	5½ miles (8.8km)
•MINIMUM TIME•	2hrs 30min
•ASCENT / GRADIENT•	110ft (34m)
•LEVEL OF DIFFICULTY•	
•PATHS•	Field tracks, former railway line, pavements, 4 stiles
•LANDSCAPE•	Parkland, arable fields, common and valley
•SUGGESTED MAP•	aqua3 OS Explorer 182 St Albans & Hatfield
•START / FINISH•	Grid reference: TL 132140
•DOG FRIENDLINESS•	Lots of other dogs in Rothamsted Park; care on golf course
•PARKING•	Amenbury Lane car park, Harpenden
•PUBLIC TOILETS•	Harpenden Leisure Centre and St Albans Road at B652

BACKGROUND TO THE WALK

Harpenden grew out of Westminster Abbey's gradual clearing of woodland for farming and settlement within its Wheathampstead manor, granted by Edward the Confessor in 1060. The first reference to a parish church is in 1221 and the town probably grew up around then. It has a striking plan, standing at the tip of a vast, triangular common over a mile (1.6km) long, and given more definition by 20th-century development along both edges. The common narrows down to a tree-lined grassy bank south of the church. There are some fine, Georgian houses spreading southwards from the town alongside the north part. The arrival of the railway and the sale of farms for residential development after 1880 radically changed Harpenden's surroundings and around 30,000 people live in Harpenden today. Nevertheless, the town's core remains intact and, within a few minutes, you can be out in countryside in Rothamsted Park or on the common.

The parish church of St Nicholas is prominent in the townscape. The church's Purbeck marble font is from about 1200 and the west tower is 15th century. Further south, the former Bull Inn, now No 27 Leyton Road, is a 15th-century, timber-framed hall house. It had been an inn since before 1586. The George pub at No 4 High Street has been on the site since at least 1507.

Close to Harpenden is Rothamsted Park. It is now part of the renowned Institute of Arable Crop Research, formerly Rothamsted Experimental Station. In front of its main building, which faces the common, is a stone, erected in 1893, commemorating 50 years of experiments by Sir John Bennet Lawes and Joseph Henry Gilbert. Lawes inherited the Rothamsted estate in 1834. Eight years later he patented a phosphate fertiliser, the sales of which enriched him immensely. With the proceeds he started the experimental station, building laboratories in the 1850s. He set up the Rothamsted Trust in 1889. The architectural centrepiece of the estate is Rothamsted Manor which, unfortunately, is only glimpsed from the walk. In 1623 the Wittewronge family, originally from Flanders, bought the estate, having leased it since 1611. By 1659 Sir John Wittewronge had built extensions and made many alterations to the medieval core, among which – we should not be surprised – was the addition of Dutch gables! For once the windows were not later replaced by sliding sashes and the house appears much as it must have done to Sir John in 1659.

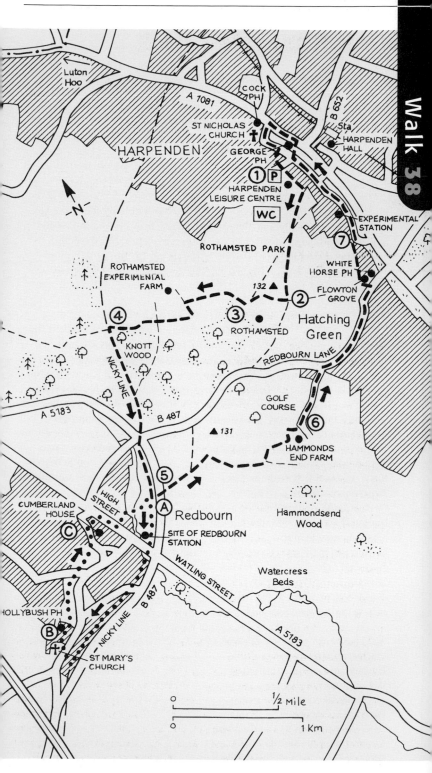

Luton Hoo

A 1081

COCK PH

St NICHOLAS CHURCH

HARPENDEN

GEORGE PH

① P

HARPENDEN LEISURE CENTRE

WC

B 652

Sta

HARPENDEN HALL

EXPERIMENTAL STATION

⑦

ROTHAMSTED PARK

ROTHAMSTED EXPERIMENTAL FARM

132 ▲

②

FLOWTON GROVE

WHITE HORSE PH

③ ROTHAMSTED

Hatching Green

N

④

KNOTT WOOD

NICKY LINE

REDBOURN LANE

A 5183

B 487

▲ 131

GOLF COURSE

⑥

HAMMONDS END FARM

⑤

HIGH STREET

Ⓐ Redbourn

CUMBERLAND HOUSE

Ⓒ

SITE OF REDBOURN STATION

Hammondsend Wood

WATLING STREET

Watercress Beds

HOLLYBUSH PH

Ⓑ

NICKY LINE

B 487

A 5183

St MARY'S CHURCH

0   ½ mile

0   1 Km

Walk 38 Directions

① From the **Amenbury Lane car park**, go right, into **Hay Lane**. Past the **Harpenden Leisure Centre** enter the park and follow the path to a lime avenue. Turn right and continue along this lime avenue to a T-junction.

② Turn right here into another lime avenue. After four trees go right, through a gate at a bridleway sign, and head diagonally right to a gate in the far corner.

WHILE YOU'RE THERE ⓘ
Why not visit **Luton Hoo** just over the Bedfordshire border and 3½ mile (5.7km) north west of Harpenden? Famous for its Russian Imperial art, jewellery and porcelain collections, it was remodelled for the diamond magnate, Sir Julius Wernher.

③ Look left for views of Rothamsted Park's clusters of chimneys and gables before turning right to join a lane. When the road turns right towards **Rothamsted Experimental Farm** go left on a tarmac track and then right at a bridleway sign, the path now a grassy margin. Continue across a lane on to a path between arable fields and follow it as it curves left down to **Knott Wood**. Walk alongside it and, out of the field, turn left on to the **Nicky Line** path.

④ The path follows the course of this former railway line to the **Harpenden Road**. Cross the road, skirt to the left of the roundabout and go up the right-hand side of the **A5183** – there is a Nicky Line sign. The path regains the trackbed. Just past the gates to a gypsy site go left over a stile to cross the **A5183**.

(This is Point Ⓐ, where Walk 39 diverges to continue along the railway path.)

⑤ Over the main road climb some steps to a stile. Continue across an arable field, with electricity poles to your left. Go through a hedge gap and straight on, then bear right. The path goes into an overgrown green lane, shortly with a golf course to your left. Pass behind the 8th tee and turn left along the golf course side of the hedge. Past the ninth tee turn right, the path winding through scrub. Beyond this cross a stile and some pasture, bypassing **Hammonds End Farm**.

⑥ Turn left along the lane then right on to **Redbourn Lane**. At the White Horse pub go left by **Flowton Green**, then turn right on to a footpath to the left of **Flowton Grove**. Beyond a thatched cottage you reach the road along the west side of **Harpenden Common**.

⑦ Turn left and walk past the **Institute of Arable Crop Research**. Continue alongside **West Common** into **Harpenden**. Go along the **High Street** to Church Green and the parish church. From here walk south to **Leyton Green**. Finally turn right into **Amenbury Road** and the car park.

WHAT TO LOOK FOR ⓘ
The **Nicky Line** is the nickname of the Hemel Hempstead to Harpenden railway. It was started in 1866 and finally opened in 1877, hauling Redbourn out of the doldrums caused by the loss of its coaching trade. It closed to passengers in 1947, but survived for freight until 1979 when the trackbed was bought by the county council. The origins of the nickname are obscure, but it may be after St Nicholas' Church in Harpenden.

Along the Line to Redbourn

Go that extra mile (or two) to the superb Church of St Mary.
See map and information panel for Walk 38

•DISTANCE•	2 miles (3.2km)
•MINIMUM TIME•	1hr
•ASCENT / GRADIENT•	25ft (8m) ▲▲ ▲▲ ▲▲
•LEVEL OF DIFFICULTY•	👫 👫 👫

Walk 39 Directions
(Walk 38 option)

From Point Ⓐ continue along the **Nicky Line**, passing the site of **Redbourn Station** on your right, it's now a picnic area. Cross **Watling Street** on a bridge with a view along Redbourn's **High Street**.

Continue along the old railway. The bridge across **Chequer Lane** is missing, so you must descend to cross the road. Further along, ignore a footpath up some steps to the left. Leave the railway at the next footpath post, going right, over a stile, to descend between gardens. At the road turn right and then into the **parish churchyard**, Point Ⓑ.

St Mary's Church is basically Norman with a north aisle added around 1140. Unusually, much of the later medieval work is precisely dated from documents: the south east chapel with its brick parapet (1448–55); the nave clerestory (1478) and the north aisle (rebuilt in 1497). Inside the rood screen was installed and painted in 1478–9.

Head eastwards from the church, along a lime avenue to the churchyard gates. Church End has

18th-century cottages, a former workhouse (rebuilt in 1790) and the Hollybush pub. Although Redbourn is surrounded by housing estates, Church End to the west and Street End to the east are linked by a large common.

From **Church End** lane bear left to walk within a lime avenue across **West Common**. Near the eastern end of this common bear left at a footpath fork to head for its north eastern corner, Point Ⓒ. You will come to **Cumberland House**, a fine, red brick, Georgian house. Go down **Lamb Lane** then turn right at a footpath signed 'High Street'.

At the **High Street** turn right. Just past the **Red House** go left into **Waterend Lane**, initially between high, brick boundary walls. Where the tarmac swings left carry straight on, the lane curving right across a ford. The lane becomes a footpath past some steel bollards. Carry straight on and descend steps to rejoin the **Nicky Line** at Point Ⓐ.

WHERE TO EAT AND DRINK ℹ

Towards the end of the walk, at Hatching Green, is the **White Horse**. In Harpenden itself, you are spoilt for choice. Try the **Cock**, the **Cross Keys** or the **George** in the High Street, or the **Oak Tree**, facing Leyton Green.

Walk 40

Kings Langley's Lost Legacy

A walk from Kings Langley and back along the Grand Union Canal.

•DISTANCE•	6½ miles (10.4km)
•MINIMUM TIME•	2hrs 30min
•ASCENT / GRADIENT•	220ft (67m) ▲▲ ▲ ▲
•LEVEL OF DIFFICULTY•	🚶🚶 🚶🚶 🚶🚶
•PATHS•	Field paths, bridleways and canal tow path, 9 stiles
•LANDSCAPE•	Chalk hills and dry valleys westwards; Gade Valley and Grand Union Canal eastwards
•SUGGESTED MAP•	aqua3 OS Explorer 182 St Albans & Hatfield
•START / FINISH•	Grid reference: TL 071026
•DOG FRIENDLINESS•	Cattle in fields around Langley Lodge are main concern; some pony paddocks elsewhere
•PARKING•	Car park on Langley Hill, west of High Street
•PUBLIC TOILETS•	Off Kings Langley High Street, down footpath beside Saracens Free House pub, opposite Langley Hill junction

Walk 40 Directions

From the car park walk up **Langley Hill**. Turn left into **Archer Close**. Go right on to a signposted footpath, initially between garden fences and then with fields on the left and the **Rudolf Steiner School** on the right. The path curves right to a stile, then runs along a road, turning left to cross the **A41**.

Descend the hill (with housing on the right) and, opposite No 102, go left over a stile into pasture. Follow the hedge south through five pastures, descending to a valley

---

WHERE TO EAT AND DRINK ⓘ

There is some choice in Kings Langley. Try the **Taste of India** tandoori restaurant, next to the **Saracens Free House**. The footpath adjacent to this Tudor pub is called (and has been since before 1389) 'Dronken Lane'. At Hunton Bridge the **King's Head** and the **Dog and Partridge** are across the canal bridge.

---

bottom. Turn left before a stile (do not climb it) to follow a hedged path, then go over a stile and turn right on to a green lane. Pass some farm buildings on your right. At a footpath sign turn right, with the boundary wall to **Langley Lodge** alongside and **Berry Bush Farmhouse** on your right.

Follow the concrete road to the left, with a pond to your right. Turn right, guided by a painted sign on a farm building, to go over a stile and straight on in a cattle pasture. Ignore a left turn and carry on alongside a fence. Go through a gate and continue along the right-hand side of the fence, descending steeply to the valley bottom. Go uphill through a hedge, then head diagonally left across arable land, towards a group of trees. Pass a gate and turn left on to a green lane, signposted 'Langleybury Lane'. This follows the parish boundary downhill, back into the valley. Beyond a gate the bridleway swings right to follow the valley bottom. Ignore paths meeting and crossing the lane. Continue as it goes left to climb out of the valley between hedges. At the crest pass **Model Farm**. Beyond it the track becomes a tarmac lane within a lime avenue. Passing through woods, the lane crosses the **M25**.

At the road turn left and walk downhill. On the right is **Langleybury House**, which is now a school, its farm a Hertfordshire County Council children's farm. The mansion was built in the 1720s for the then Lord Chief Justice, Sir Robert Raymond. It is an early Georgian, four-square building in brick with a balustraded parapet and urns. You get a good view of its north east front as you descend to **Hunton Bridge**. Pass **St Paul's Church**, built in flint and stone bands by Henry Woodyer in 1865.

Cross the busy **A41** into **Bridge Road**. Past the brick and flint former school of 1858, turn left before the bridge to descend to the **Grand Union Canal** tow path. Follow it north through the water-meadows of the **River Gade**, past **Lock 71**, North Grove. Pass under the **M25** viaduct, a rather graceful curving one on channelled piers. Continue past **Lock 70** and then a boating lake on the left. Go past the

> **WHAT TO LOOK FOR** ⓘ
> Passing under the M25, as you walk along the canal tow path, you'll see a microcosm of **transport history**, spanning nearly 2,000 years. All these routes make use of the Gade Valley: the A41/A4251 following a Roman road, turnpiked in the 18th century; the canal of 1797; the railway of 1837; and the M25, this time crossing the valley on its fine viaduct of 1986.

large 1930 Ovaltine factory along the opposite bank. Leave the canal at a road bridge. Turn left on to the road that bears left and then right uphill, now **Church Lane**, to Kings Langley's parish church. On the right you'll see **Church House** built in 1805 as a brewery maltings but now offices.

> **WHILE YOU'RE THERE** ⓘ
> How the mighty are fallen! A visit to **Cassiobury Park** south of Hunton Bridge, is a sobering experience. West of the Grand Union Canal it's now a golf course, to the east a lovely public park for Watford citizens. The grand 1670s mansion of Arthur Capell, Earl of Essex was completely demolished in 1927.

The medieval parish church contains the ornate tomb of Edmund of Langley, Duke of York and Edward III's fifth son, born at Langley Palace in 1341. The alabaster tomb was brought here from Langley Friary in 1575. The royal connection goes back a little further. Kings Langley's palace was built around 1286 by Edward I. Edward II founded a Franciscan friary near by and his favourite, Piers Gaveston, was buried here after his murder in 1312. After 1500 the palace fell into decay and little survives. The site of the palace is within the Rudolph Steiner School's grounds. The friary survives in part though, a building 76ft (23m) long by 18ft (5.5m) wide.

From the church turn right into the **High Street**. This has many worthy buildings, some timber-framed Tudor and 17th-century, mostly refronted in brick. It retains much of Kings Langley's character as an old coaching town. Beyond the **Saracens Free House** turn left, back into **Langley Hill**.

The Long and Straight Road From Markyate to Flamstead

A walk along Watling Street, returning along the chalky ridge.

•DISTANCE•	7 miles (11.3km)
•MINIMUM TIME•	3hrs
•ASCENT / GRADIENT•	175ft (53m) ▲ ▲ ▲
•LEVEL OF DIFFICULTY•	👫 👫 👫
•PATHS•	Tracks, field paths, some roads, 5 stiles
•LANDSCAPE•	Chalk ridges on either side of young Ver's valley
•SUGGESTED MAP•	aqua3 OS Explorer 182 St Albans & Hatfield
•START / FINISH•	Grid reference: TL 059166
•DOG FRIENDLINESS•	Mostly arable country but sheep pasture south west of Markyate, care also needed on Watling Street
•PARKING•	On Markyate High Street
•PUBLIC TOILETS•	None on route

BACKGROUND TO THE WALK

The long and narrow Markyate High Street is set out along Roman Watling Street. The town prospered in the 18th and earlier 19th century from the coach trade – it had several inns, being half-way between St Albans and Dunstable. On the High Street you will see a mixture of properties. Many are Georgian, many are 19th-century brick-fronted houses, and, particularly at the north end, you will find several 16th- and 17th-century, timber-framed ones. The houses on the east side of the High Street had long narrow closes, up to 200yds (183m) long. Sadly these were largely destroyed by the 1957 bypass which, admittedly, relieved the choked High Street.

Strange Lady

In the Middle Ages Markyate was famed for 'the Lady Christina of the Woods', a recluse living in the woods near by. She was the first prioress of the Priory of the Holy Trinity, founded in 1145. The Benedictine nunnery lay on the site of the oddly-named Markyate Cell, the mansion north of the town set in delightful parkland along the River Ver. It is seen from the churchyard of St John the Baptist's, a part-1734, plum brick church. A plaque on the nave reads 'This Chapel Enlarged by Jos Howell AD 1811', the then owner of Markyate Cell. The priory was dissolved in 1537 and the site was granted to Humphrey Bourchier. He demolished much of it and converted it into a house. Other alterations were made later, including those by the Ferrers family, but much of its present, Elizabethan appearance is due to Robert Lugar's 1820s rebuildings and alterations for Daniel Goodson Adey of St Albans. Yet more rebuilding was undertaken after a fire in 1840.

Wicked Lady

Another lady was renowned in Markyate, but she was decidedly less virtuous. She was Kathleen Ferrers, 'the Wicked Lady of Markyate Cell'. Born in 1634, she took to highway robbery along Watling Street. Eventually she was mortally wounded in a hold-up and crawled back to Markyate Cell to die. Her ghost, draped in a black cape, has supposedly been seen on Watling Street and was blamed for three fires that severely damaged Markyate Cell.

In Memory of Children

Flamstead village, at the other end of the walk, was once a small market town. It's on a ridge overlooking the Roman road and the Ver Valley. Its church is well worth visiting, firstly for its medieval wall-paintings, which were covered over until the 1930s, and secondly for the moving Saunders Children monument of 1690, which was carved by the great William Stanton. The church is only open on Sunday afternoons between July and September. The Saunders family owned Beechwood Park, a mansion built on the site of another Benedictine nunnery, St Giles-in-the-Wood, which was dissolved in 1537. Thomas Saunders built the almshouses to the north of the church, as well as commissioning this superb monument.

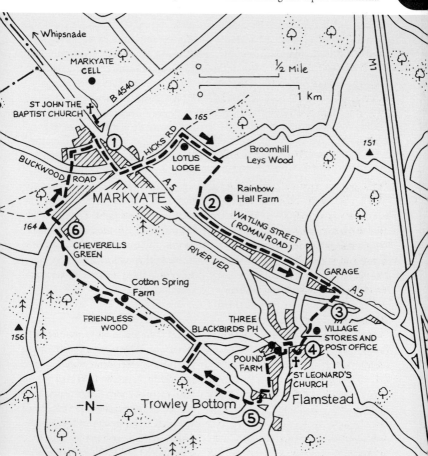

Walk 41 Directions

① From the north end of Markyate **High Street** walk southwards. Turn left into **Hicks Road**, crossing the

A5 on a footbridge. Past **Lotus Lodge** turn right. Where the lane turns left, go straight on along a green lane which shortly turns right to descend, through seemingly perpetual mud, to the valley road.

② Turn left on to the course of the Roman road, **Watling Street**, a stretch now bypassed. Follow this for over a mile (1.6km) until, at a petrol station, you turn right to cross the A5.

③ Once over a stile head diagonally right, across a stream to another stile. Follow the field edge before heading into a copse that climbs the valley side. Emerging from this copse, climb a stile to go left alongside a hedge. Cross another stile and head to a lane, **River Hill**, which leads into **Flamstead**.

WHERE TO EAT AND DRINK ⓘ
Markyate has a number of pubs, some of which are former coaching inns. In the High Street are the **Swan**, the **Sun Inn** and the **Red Lion**. In London Road you'll find the **Plume of Feathers**. There's also a **tandoori restaurant** and a **fish and chip shop**. Flamstead has the **Three Blackbirds** pub (and a **village store**).

---

④ At the junction turn left along **High Street**, right into **Church Lane** and then right again, into the parish churchyard. Leave via a gate by the war memorial cross. Turn left along High Street and then left into **Trowley Hill Road**. Beyond No 30, **Pound Farm**, turn right on to a tarmac path, signposted 'The Chiltern Way'. At a footpath post

---

WHAT TO LOOK FOR ⓘ
Markyate Cell, the mansion named after the medieval nunnery, is best seen on this walk from beside the parish church. It sits on the opposite side of the Ver Valley in rolling parkland with fine mature sycamores, horse chestnuts and limes. You could not pretend that the house is beautiful. It's an overblown Elizabethan-style 19th century near rebuild of a much altered Tudor mansion, but it is certainly characterful and robust.

WHILE YOU'RE THERE ⓘ
Five miles north west of Markyate, is **Whipsnade Zoo**, the out-station of the Zoological Society of London, where animals have considerably more freedom than in London Zoo itself. Now also called Whipsnade Wild Animal Park, it was very much a pioneer of free-range zoo-keeping when it opened in 1931. South of the Dunstable Downs escarpment, there are over 2,500 animals in its 600 acres (243ha).

---

turn left and descend along the edge of an arable field. At the bottom of the field go left between some gardens to a lane and turn right.

⑤ At **Trowley Bottom** go straight on, then immediately right on to a bridleway, at first behind cottages, then along the valley. At a lane turn right to climb out of the valley. At the crest turn left. At a footpath sign, 'Cheverells Green', bear left into **Friendless Wood**. Once out of the wood go right. The path then follows the ridge along the edge of this and another wood before heading through a series of kissing gates and sheep pasture to rejoin the lane.

⑥ Go left to the junction, turn right, then left to a footpath sign, 'Buckwood Road'. At a footpath junction turn right and walk alongside an arable field and gardens to a road. Across it the path climbs between gardens. Go along **Cowper Road** to **Cavendish Road** junction. Here you turn right, descending to Markyate **High Street**. Turn left and, just before the **White Hart Inn**, go right to the subway under the A5. Turn left to visit the church (from its churchyard you can see Markyate Cell house). Retrace your steps to the **High Street**.

Fields of Great Gaddesden

A walk entirely within the richly rewarding parish of Great Gaddesden.

Walk 42

·DISTANCE·	6 miles (9.7km)
·MINIMUM TIME·	3hrs
·ASCENT / GRADIENT·	240ft (73m) ▲ ▲ ▲
·LEVEL OF DIFFICULTY·	🚶 🚶 🚶
·PATHS·	Field paths and bridleways, 37 stiles
·LANDSCAPE·	Water-meadows and plateau above
·SUGGESTED MAP·	aqua3 OS Explorer 182 St Albans & Hatfield
·START / FINISH·	Grid reference: TL 030137
·DOG FRIENDLINESS·	Often on leads – many cattle, sheep, horses and ponies
·PARKING·	The Green, Jockey End
·PUBLIC TOILETS·	None on route

BACKGROUND TO THE WALK

The sparkling upper waters of the River Gade wind through damp, green water-meadows, the valley rising on both sides to the chalk plateau. Human impact on the landscape here is very ancient. Up on the plateau above the valley is a pattern of long, narrow, rectangular fields. It seems to be the remains of the Roman grid field system known as 'centuriation' (division into hundreds). It was laid out to the north and north west of the Roman town of Verulamium (St Albans, ▶ Walk 35), possibly in the late 1st century AD.

Centuriation: When and Why?

A close look at the Ordanance Survey map shows the pattern very strongly in the area between Jockey Row and Golden Parsonage, the route of our walk. It is particularly clear here because the fields remain pastoral. In Redbourn, Flamstead, Bedmond and elsewhere it is less obvious because many hedges have been grubbed out to make more profitable arable fields. There are three explanations in circulation for the field system. One theory is that 'centuriation' took place after Boudica, the fiery Queen of the Iceni, sacked Verulamium in AD 60; a second is that the highly Romanised aristocracy of the local Catuvellauni tribe reorganised their estates in the Roman way; and a third sees the field system as merely refining pre-Roman, Belgic or Catuvellauni, colonisation. Whatever the case, the field boundaries are either at right angles to, or parallel to, the Roman road system. This is particular clear with Watling Street and the road that runs south west from St Albans, along the southern edge of the Chilterns. Gaddesden Row looks like any other country lane but the map shows it aligned parallel to Watling Street and a key element in the Roman field pattern. It is awe-inspiring to think that these fields had their boundaries established nearly 2,000 years ago.

Golden Parks

Parks were laid out on top of this ancient landscape and you will pass three of them on this walk – Gaddesden Place, The Hoo and Golden Parsonage. The 'golden' in Golden Parsonage is a corruption of 'Gaddesden'. This park has several surviving late 17th-century sweet chestnuts. A tree ring count of a fallen tree showed its avenue of limes (leading towards the house from London Wood) to be over three centuries old. The house was built in 1705 for John Halsey. Earlier sets of buildings ranges were demolished when the Halseys moved to their new mansion, Gaddesden Place (encountered earlier on the route). The Halseys employed James Wyatt to design Gaddesden Place in 1768, but it was extensively rebuilt after a disastrous fire in 1905. 'Capability' Brown's The Hoo parkland also partially survives but its house was also extensively rebuilt (around 1904).

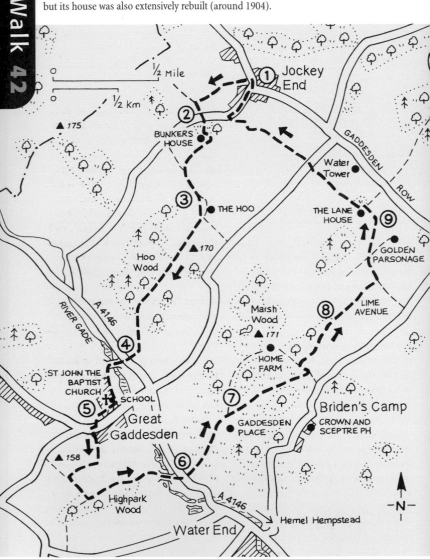

Walk 42 Directions

① From **The Green** go past the bus shelter and turn left at a footpath sign into paddocks. Walk alongside the hedge. Where it ends cross to a hedge. Turn left, then pass through oak and thorn scrub to a road.

② Cross the road on to the **Bunkers House** drive, bearing left at its gates. Go over a stile to walk alongside the garden hedge, then cross a cultivated field to a stile. Go through the hedge and turn left.

③ Cross a stile by a large oak, then head diagonally to the right of **The Hoo**, a house in remnants of 18th-century parkland. Follow the fence towards the woods, then enter them. From the woods descend across some arable land to a hedge, following the field edge as it curves right to a road by some houses.

WHERE TO EAT AND DRINK ⓘ

The only pub near the route is the **Crown and Sceptre** at Briden's Camp. To visit it necessitates a slight diversion after you have passed Gaddesden Place.

---

④ Cross into some water-meadows. Walk across the long footbridge, then bear left towards the parish church. Beyond the Victorian, brick and flint school, turn right to enter the churchyard.

⑤ From the south west corner of the churchyard, cross some pasture to a road. Turn right, then go left at a footpath sign by some cottages. In the field, head to a stile, go over it and follow a grass margin to some arable land. Turn right at the crest. At a footpath T-junction turn left to head for some woods. Once in them turn immediately left, the path

---

WHAT TO LOOK FOR ⓘ

Browsing **church memorials** often gives glimpses up fascinating historical byways or of the interesting lives of those commemorated. In Great Gaddesden church seek out those to Thomas Plumer Halsey and his wife and son, all drowned in the Mediterranean when the steamship *Ercolano* sunk in 1854, or Dorothy Abdy who left an annual grant of tea and sugar to eight local widows.

WHILE YOU'RE THERE ⓘ

About 3 miles (4.8km) to the south of Great Gaddesden you'll find the sprawling New Town of **Hemel Hempstead**. Despite its 'anytown' feel, it also possesses one of Hertfordshire's best churches. Set between parkland by the River Gade and the old town's High Street, St Mary's is almost entirely Norman, with a soaring spire, an aisled nave and stone rib vaulted chancel.

---

descending to the valley. At a stile bear right to a footbridge and then go between buildings to a road.

⑥ Go through a gate beside some cottages, climb a stile, and turn left, uphill, across cultivated land towards the porticoed **Gaddesden Place**. Go into parkland, climb two stiles, and head uphill, to the left of an oak and then to a waymarker post to the left of the mansion.

⑦ Past Gaddesden Place and through a field gate, head to a drinking trough. Bear right to a stile by some woods, then head to a gate. Turn left on to a metalled track to **Home Farm**. At the wood edge go right at a footpath sign to walk beside the wood.

⑧ The path then enters **Golden Parsonage**'s ancient lime avenue. Leave this at the valley bottom by turning left on to a track. At a track junction go right and immediately diagonally left towards a stile, passing ancient sweet chestnuts, to another stile.

⑨ Once over this, continue through a sequence of paddocks and stiles, passing **The Lane House**, crossing a road and continuing north west, passing a copse. Beyond the copse you reach a road, turn right here, back to **Jockey End**.

Ashridge's Wedding Cake

A walk in Ashridge Park and the wooded commons of the Chiltern plateau.

•DISTANCE•	6½ miles (10.4km)
•MINIMUM TIME•	3hrs
•ASCENT / GRADIENT•	225ft (69m) ▲▲ ▲
•LEVEL OF DIFFICULTY•	🚶🚶 🚶🚶 🚶
•PATHS•	Mostly tracks through woodland or parkland
•LANDSCAPE•	Beechwoods, parkland and golf course on chalk plateau
•SUGGESTED MAP•	aqua3 OS Explorer 181 Chiltern Hills North
•START / FINISH•	Grid reference: SP 976128
•DOG FRIENDLINESS•	On lead crossing golf course
•PARKING•	Car park on Aldbury Common, on road to Bridgewater Monument
•PUBLIC TOILETS•	At Bridgewater Monument visitor centre (seasonal)

BACKGROUND TO THE WALK

Once described as a 'wedding cake', Ashridge is the centrepiece of this walk, a great, early 19th-century Gothic palace. It is set on the eastern edge of a heavily wooded chalk plateau. To its western side is the Aldbury escarpment and to the east is a descent into the deeply cut 'Golden Valley'. Although its grounds were landscaped by Lancelot 'Capability' Brown in the 1760s and by Humphrey Repton after 1800, much of the effect stems from the dense woodland to the west and south, including the medieval woodland commons of Aldbury, Berkhamsted and, over the county boundary, Ivinghoe.

Fairy-tale Palace

The mansion bursts from this woodland like a fairy-tale palace. It is built in Totternhoe stone, a white and greyish chalkstone that was quarried over the border in Bedfordshire. James Wyatt designed Ashridge in 1808. His son Jeffry, who Frenchified his name to 'Wyatville', added more from 1814 to 1820. Views are dominated by the more ornate chapel tower and the main block at the east end that almost resembles a castle keep. This great, romantic, rambling mansion was not the first house on the site, however, for there was a medieval monastic college of Augustinian canons here, one of two Colleges of Bonshommes in England, the other being at Edington in Wiltshire. It was founded by Edmund, Earl of Cornwall, a nephew of Henry III in 1275, to look after a holy relic, a phial allegedly containing some of the blood of Christ. Only a cellar or vaulted undercroft survives, its stone vaults supported by octagonal columns. At 68ft (20.7m) long by 26ft (7.9m) wide it is quite a substantial fragment.

After the Dissolution of the monasteries under Henry VIII the college became a secular mansion (set in a deer park) and Edward VI spent much of his short life here before becoming King in 1547 (as did his sister, later Queen Elizabeth I).

The Duke of Bridgewater, who commissioned 'Capability' Brown to rework the park, also consulted Sir William Chambers over rebuilding the old house. This was not implemented, but the Golden Valley plantings and much of Brown's work survives, albeit further changed by the modern golf course through which the walk passes.

The Prince's Riding

One of the most spectacular historic landscape features seen on this walk is the Prince's Riding, a great cut taken out of the woodland, part of which was Aldbury Common. This was done to give Ashridge a view of the 1832 Bridgewater Monument (► Walk 49), 1½ miles (2.4km) away. The house has now come full circle: from a great landowner's mansion it has reverted to collegiate status, albeit secular, as a management training college.

Walk 43 **Directions**

① From the car park on **Aldbury Common** head towards the distinctive column of the

Bridgewater Monument, turning left at a footpath sign behind a young beech tree. Keep straight on along this track until, just before a pond, go left by a footpath post at a track crossroads.

Walk 43

② On reaching a road, cross on to a byway. The woodland gives way on the left to parkland with cattle grazing. The track bears right into woodland, skirting a paddock and **Woodyard Cottages**, to reach a metalled track. Follow it to the right, still within woodland. At a footpath crossroads, before a gate to some farm buildings, go left on to a track. At a track fork bear left and, reaching a field, follow the path that descends along the right-hand edge of the woods to a tree belt and then runs through it to a road.

③ Turn left on the road and, past the ornate **Berkhamstead Lodge**, bear right at a footpath sign, to climb through woodland. At the crest walk alongside some wire fencing and the grounds of **Ashridge College**.

④ Turn right. With an oak copse on your left, head for a footpath sign to the left of a large oak. Now you get good views of Ashridge. Cross the drive and follow the white-topped posts across **Prince's**

Riding, a vista terminated by the Bridgewater Monument. Continue through a copse and follow more white posts. Cross a dry valley and then the golf practice range. Beyond the practice tees the path winds through a copse to a road.

⑤ Turn right along the road, now the **Chiltern Way**. Where it turns left, the footpath bears right between garden hedges, across a fairway, then between more gardens and past the gate to **Witches Hollow**. At a footpath crossroads (Point Ⓐ, where the longer Walk 44 diverges and rejoins) turn left on to a metalled track.

⑥ Follow the metalled lane downhill. Past the drive to **Witchcraft Hill** it becomes a path through woods. Over a stile the path bears left alongside a clearing, then into some woods to the road at **Ringshall**.

⑦ Turn left here and, immediately past some garden walls, turn right into the woods of **Ivinghoe Common**. At a bridleway post bear left, then left again to walk along a ride, ignoring all tracks and paths to left or right. Eventually you cross a dry valley and, at a bridleway post where the track bears right, go almost straight on to wind through the wood to **Prince's Riding** and the car park.

Little Gaddesden

Walk a little further to visit Little Gaddesden and its memorials.
See map and information panel for Walk 43

•DISTANCE•	1 mile (1.6km)
•MINIMUM TIME•	30min
•ASCENT / GRADIENT•	Negligible
•LEVEL OF DIFFICULTY•	

Walk 44 **Directions** (Walk 43 option)

From Point Ⓐ, instead of turning left on to the metalled track, go straight on along a footpath, with a close-boarded fence on the left, and a post-and-net fence on the right with a paddock beyond. Go over a stile and you are in the car park to the **Bridgewater Arms** pub (opened in 1815). The arms are those of the Egertons, the Earls and Dukes of Bridgewater of Ashridge, whose memorials you will see shortly in Little Gaddesden church.

At the road turn right. Go left, opposite the refronted Nos 15–17 (a 17th-century house), through a kissing gate on to a path between post-and-rail fences and paddocks, now on the waymarked **Chiltern Way**. Bear left between fences with bungalow gardens on the right. Through a gate cross a pasture diagonally left, to leave it over a stile. Cross over a lane to another stile, then head diagonally to a further stile. Climb this and bear left to follow the right-hand side of the hedge. At the field corner go through a kissing gate. Cross this paddock to a stile. Go over a lane to enter the churchyard, Point Ⓑ.

St Peter and St Paul Church is situated in splendid isolation, well away from the village. Its churchyard is fringed with pines, oaks and firs, while shaped yew bushes ornament the churchyard itself. The church has battlemented parapets and the oldest parts are 15th-century. The major interest inside is in the south east chapel. Here you will find the Bridgewater Mausoleum, built in 1819 by Jeffry Wyatville (► Background to Walk 43). It is filled with wall monuments to the Earls and Dukes of Bridgewater, including the canal-building third Duke whose monument is seen on Walks 43 and 49. Wyatville also rebuilt the south aisle and added the porch.

From the churchyard go through a kissing gate between the churchyard hedge and the car park. Through another kissing gate continue straight on through pasture. Go over two stiles and through two more kissing gates to a road. Turn left and walk through the village, passing a shop and post office. Reaching the **Bridgewater Arms** again, turn right into its car park, over the stile and along the footpath to rejoin the route of Walk 43, turning right on to the metalled track at the footpath crossroads of Point Ⓐ.

Walk 45

Berkhamsted's Great Castle

View the castle and return along the Grand Union Canal.

•DISTANCE•	5 miles (8km)
•MINIMUM TIME•	2hrs 30min
•ASCENT / GRADIENT•	235ft (72m) ▲ ▲ ▲
•LEVEL OF DIFFICULTY•	🚶 🚶 🚶
•PATHS•	Pavements, field paths and canal tow path, 2 stiles
•LANDSCAPE•	Valley and rolling chalk hills
•SUGGESTED MAP•	aqua3 OS Explorer 181 Chiltern Hills North
•START / FINISH•	Grid reference: SP 990079
•DOG FRIENDLINESS•	Off leads except in town
•PARKING•	Lower Kings Road car park, Berkhamsted
•PUBLIC TOILETS•	Water Lane car park, Berkhamsted

Walk 45 Directions

From the car park turn left into the **High Street**, passing the former town hall of 1859, now a trendy café. At **Market Square** the road divides – go down the left-hand, cobbled alley to the church and the 16th-century, timber-framed **Court House** by the churchyard gates. The parish church is a large one. It has an Early English chancel and crossing (from around AD 1200) surmounted by a 1536 tower. Turn left into **Castle Street**, past the 1544 building of **Berkhamsted School**, a grammar school founded by John Incent, Dean of St Paul's Cathedral in London. Once across the canal turn right into **Station Road**, then left opposite the **Crystal Palace** pub

---

WHERE TO EAT AND DRINK ⓘ

There is plenty of choice in the way of pubs, cafés and restaurants in Berkhamsted. For bar meals in historic surroundings, look for the the **Bull** and the **King's Arms** in the High Street, or the **Crystal Palace** on Station Road. In Northchurch try the **George and Dragon**.

---

under the railway bridge and left again to skirt the castle.

The siege of Berkhamsted Castle in 1216 followed the civil war between King John and his barons after the signing of Magna Carta at Runnymede in 1215. The barons had unwisely called on King Philip Augustus of France for help. He sent his son, Louis le Dauphin, and a French army. They ravaged Hertfordshire, capturing both Berkhamsted and Hertford castles and occupied St Albans before being ousted in 1217.

From the castle head towards the station and turn right to **Brownlow Road**. Where the road bears right carry straight on into **Castle Hill**, then straight on over a stile to the right of Berkhamsted Cricket Sports and Social Club's access road. Through a car park you pass tennis courts and a cricket pavilion, the route becoming a track. Over a stile continue to a footpath sign just past an electricity pole and go through a kissing gate. Turn left to follow a hedge alongside an arable field, climbing steeply out of the dry valley. Go through a hedge gap, with the path still along the right side of the hedge, the ascent is now more gentle. The track bears left to another hedge gap and you continue, now on the chalk plateau, to a further hedge gap. Aim for the tree belt ahead, the hedge now vestigial. At the tree belt turn left and follow it downhill. Ahead, across the valley, Berkhamsted's conically roofed, Victorian water tower dominates the skyline. Go through a kissing gate on to a sheltered path. Turn right on to a bridleway, with a metalled track with paddocks to your left and houses to your right. Carry straight on through woods to emerge at the edge of **Northchurch Common**.

Turn left to descend the **B4506** road into **Northchurch**, crossing the canal to the main road. Turn left on to the **A4251**, which follows the course of Roman Akeman Street through the Bulbourne Valley. Pass the school to reach **St Mary's Church**, which has Anglo-Saxon work to its nave. Just past the church is a fine cluster of 16th-century cottages.

WHILE YOU'RE THERE ⓘ
Visit **Berkhamsted Castle** with its superb earthwork ramparts, moats and high keep mound, or motte. The motte is about 45ft (13.7m) high with the remains of the stone keep 60ft (18.3m) in diameter and a deep well at its summit. The first castle, including the earthwork motte and bailey, was built by William the Conqueror's half-brother Robert of Mortain after 1067, the surviving stonework all being later. From the motte summit you can look down into the bailey with remains of its 12th-century encircling stone walls and towers. Beyond are the reedy moats and further earthen ramparts.

Retrace your steps along **New Road** to the canal, joining the tow path on the south west side of the bridge beside lock Number 49, **Northchurch Lock**. Turn right and pass under Bridge 139 to follow the **Grand Union Canal**. As you pass them note Gas Locks 1 and 2, marking where Berkhamsted's gas works were serviced by the canal.

WHAT TO LOOK FOR ⓘ
Along the Grand Union Canal tow path you should see two types of **fishing**: people, often with extraordinarily long roach poles, seated along the canal banks surrounded with the modern angler's paraphernalia, or watchful herons. Large birds with their delicate grey plumage and once quite uncommon, herons can now be seen frequently, hunched and motionless on the water's edge or in the shallows watching for their prey, mostly small fish.

Berkhamsted was an important medieval town, guarding the strategic gap in the Chiltern Hills cut by the River Bulbourne. A Roman road, known to the Anglo-Saxons who later settled here as Akeman Street, passes through this important geographical cutting. The Grand Junction Canal followed it too, linking the Thames Basin with the Midlands in the 1790s. Railway builders followed in the 1830s. By the 20th century, motor traffic choked the town until the 1990s bypass.

Shortly after the **Gas Locks**, **Berkhamsted Park** is on the left, on land given by Lord Brownlow as 'compensation' for his attempted enclosure of Berkhamsted Common in 1865. Leave the canal at the iron bridge and walk up some steps. Turn right on to **Lower Kings Road** and back into **Berkhamsted**.

Delights and Surprises in Tring Park

A stimulating walk from Tring up into the wooded Chilterns and back through Tring Park.

•DISTANCE•	5½ miles (8.8km)
•MINIMUM TIME•	2hrs 30min
•ASCENT / GRADIENT•	335ft (102m) ▲▲▲
•LEVEL OF DIFFICULTY•	🚶🚶 🚶🚶 🚶🚶
•PATHS•	Pavements, footpaths, 3 stiles
•LANDSCAPE•	Arable farmland, historic parkland, woods
•SUGGESTED MAP•	aqua3 OS Explorer 181 Chiltern Hills North
•START / FINISH•	Grid reference: SP 925114
•DOG FRIENDLINESS•	Largely arable country, but horses in fields around Wigginton and cattle graze in Tring Park
•PARKING•	Car park at east end of Tring High Street (except market day, Friday)
•PUBLIC TOILETS•	At car park

BACKGROUND TO THE WALK

The quite remarkable historic parkland of Tring Park is the centrepiece of this walk. Even though construction of the A41 Tring bypass in 1974 cut it in two, many of the features shown on a 1729 map of the park have survived. The house on the north side of the bypass dates from the late 1670s. Sir Christopher Wren designed it for Henry Guy (Groom of the Bedchamber to Charles II). There is now little about it to suggest Wren's contibution because, in the 1870s, Baron Lionel Nathan de Rothschild bought the estate and added the French-style pavilion roofs and other 'enrichments'.

Leafy Avenues

With regard to the parkland, in 1705 the great Charles Bridgeman, the foremost garden and landscape designer of the day, was called in by the son of the then owner, Sir William Gore. Bridgeman planted formal, double avenues that led slightly east of south from the house towards the escarpment ridge. Although these have gone, having been replaced by less formal, later 18th- and 19th-century tree plantings, the delineation of an avenue running south west from the house survives. The trees themselves are known to have been replanted as a lime avenue in 1836, which is now interrupted by the footbridge over the bypass.

Bridgeman's 'Wilderness'

Your route enters the park from Wigginton, in woodland that is today managed by the Woodland Trust. Here you are in the south eastern corner of the park, Bridgeman's so-called 'Wilderness'. The avenues of yews and limes were laid out as long ago as the 1720s. The avenues focus on two remarkable structures, both part of the original scheme. The first you see is the Summer Pavilion or Temple. Its architect was probably James Gibbs, whose work included St Martin's in the Fields in Trafalgar Square and several garden buildings at Stowe in Buckinghamshire. The Summer Pavilion, or Temple, is just a portico with a pediment – it has no rooms behind the back wall. From here you look down an avenue to the Obelisk, also probably by Gibbs. This is supposed to be a monument to Charles II's celebrated mistress, Nell Gwynn – or possibly her dog. Beyond the Wilderness the route descends to fine parkland before the footbridge over the bypass. Leaving Tring at the start of this walk you pass the Walter Rothschild Zoological Museum, now a part of the Natural History Museum. Part of the route also follows the earthwork, Grim's Ditch (➤ Walk 48).

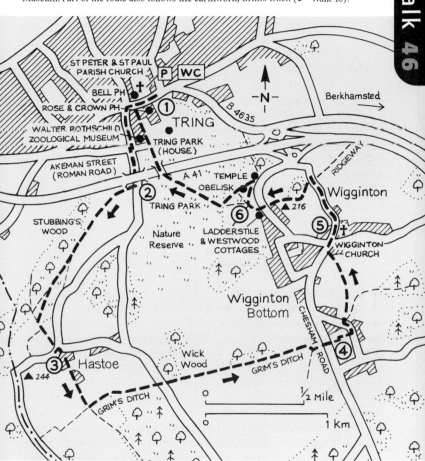

Walk 46 Directions

① Walk along the **High Street** from the car park, passing the church, to turn left at the crossroads down to **Akeman Street** and the **Walter Rothschild Zoological Museum**. At **Park Street** turn right, then go left, up **Hastoe Lane**, to climb out of Tring and under the **A41** bypass.

② Just beyond the bridge turn right at a footpath sign, 'Hastoe'. Beyond the **A41** cutting, at a gate and stile, you bear left to climb the ridge, with a hedge on your left. On reaching **Stubbing's Wood**, follow its edge initially, then enter it. At a path fork bear right – the route is marked by arrows on trees. Pass a footpath sign, 'Shire Lane Pavis Wood', then descend to a sunken

Walk 46

WHAT TO LOOK FOR ⓘ

St Peter and St Paul Church, Tring, is a large mainly 15th-century town church. This does not prepare you for the astonishingly massive and sumptuous monument to Sir William Gore of Tring Park that faces you across the nave after you enter. Gore died in 1707 and the monument, oozing smug complacency and arrogance, depicts him in his robes as Lord Mayor of London, his wife reclining beside him.

way and turn left along it. Climb towards a gateway and out of the woodland. Continue along a metalled lane. At the junction turn left, briefly on to the **Ridgeway National Trail** along **Gadmore Lane**. Leaving the Trail at a crossroads, turn right on to **Browns Lane**, a metalled bridleway.

③ Turn left at a footpath crossroads on to the **Chiltern Way**. Follow **Grim's Ditch**, with its bank and ditch, sometimes impressive and sometimes barely discernible. After about 1¼ miles (2km) go through a kissing gate on to **Chesham Road**.

④ Turn right at the road, then left through a kissing gate, still on the Chiltern Way. When you reach a lane turn left. At an electricity sub-station turn right. The Chiltern Way veers right but here you leave it, instead following the left-hand hedge, to a hedge gap and a waymarker post. Cross a dry valley

– the church belfry is visible opposite. At the hedge line head diagonally left into cattle pasture. Through a kissing gate turn right on to **Chesham Road** and proceed to **Wigginton Church**.

⑤ From the church head north along the **Twist**, winding downhill as far as the Ridgeway National Trail signs. Turn left to follow this Trail to just beyond a pair of **Rothschild** estate cottages (Ladderstile and Westwood cottages). Here the Trail turns left but you go straight on, into the woods of **Tring Park**.

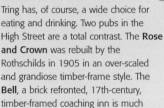

WHERE TO EAT AND DRINK ⓘ

Tring has, of course, a wide choice for eating and drinking. Two pubs in the High Street are a total contrast. The **Rose and Crown** was rebuilt by the Rothschilds in 1905 in an over-scaled and grandiose timber-frame style. The **Bell**, a brick refronted, 17th-century, timber-framed coaching inn is much more homely and welcoming.

⑥ At a cross path turn right to the **Temple** or Summer Pavilion. Head west to the **Obelisk**. Still in woodland, continue downhill to a kissing gate. Bear right here, into superb cattle-grazed, 18th-century parkland, to head for a footbridge over the **A41**. Across the bridge follow the footpath back into Tring – the route is clear, near the town being mainly between high walls – emerging in the **High Street**.

WHILE YOU'RE THERE ⓘ

In 1889, when Nathan Mayer Rothschild, First Baron Rothschild, gave his son Walter a lavish 21st birthday present he could hardly have envisaged what it would be today: the **Walter Rothschild Zoological Museum**. Housed in fine, 1890s buildings, it is one of the best such collections in the world, retaining many of the original glass cases. There are thousands of specimens – mammals, fish, birds, reptiles and insects – to see. When Walter Rothschild died in 1937 he gave it to the nation.and it is now open to the public.

Advancing on the Tring Salient

A walk on the gault clay lowlands of the Vale of Aylesbury around Long Marston and Puttenham.

•DISTANCE•	4 miles (6.4km)
•MINIMUM TIME•	2hrs
•ASCENT / GRADIENT•	Negligible
•LEVEL OF DIFFICULTY•	
•PATHS•	Field paths alongside hedges, some roads, canal tow path, 19 stiles
•LANDSCAPE•	Mixture of pasture and arable land with thorn hedges
•SUGGESTED MAP•	aqua3 OS Explorer 181 Chiltern Hills North
•START / FINISH•	Grid reference: SP 898156
•DOG FRIENDLINESS•	Dogs on leads in churchyards and around horses
•PARKING•	Along village roads in Long Marston
•PUBLIC TOILETS•	None on route

BACKGROUND TO THE WALK

Around Tring there is a curious projection of Hertfordshire into the heart of Buckinghamshire. Now thinly populated it was mostly within the parish of Tring, with only Puttenham as an independent parish. It must have been the Anglo-Saxon administrative area assigned to Tring township. Tiscott and Ardwick, in the far north of the projection, beyond Long Marston, were medieval villages that have vanished, further contributing to the 'empty quarter' feel. Up the spine of this salient is the Wingrave road from Tring that leads to more thinly populated country over the Buckinghamshire border.

Long Marston

The two villages on this walk are a complete contrast. Puttenham is little more than a hamlet while Long Marston straggles along the Wingrave road for ¹/₂ mile (800m). The core of Long Marston, however, was west along Church Lane. Although the manor house has long gone, leaving only a fragment of its moat, the tower of the original parish church remains within its churchyard.

This is the story of a church that moved. The tower is the surviving fragment of the medieval Church of All Saints. The partly Norman and later medieval church was built on a site that had became so saturated and unstable that it was downright dangerous. Its last event was a wedding in April 1882 at which only the priest, the happy couple and the witnesses were allowed in. It had been a chapel of ease to St Peter and St Paul in Tring, and only became a separate parish in 1867. All but the tower was pulled down in 1883. A new church, built on the Wingrave road in the cemetery, opened in 1870. The old churchyard had been closed in 1866 for health reasons – the mind boggles!

Much of the material from the old church was reused in the new church, but its north nave arcade came from Tring Church, which was also undergoing restoration at the time. Re-used parts include the 14th-century font, the Jacobean pulpit and various windows of the north aisle. Ironically, the gault clay under the new church proved just as unstable: major structural repairs were needed by 1907. Perhaps wisely, the great tower that had been planned was never built.

Puttenham

Across the fields the Church of St Mary, Puttenham, survives intact. Surrounded as it is by sheep-cropped pastures, it is a picture of Midland tranquillity. The church's striking 15th-century battlemented tower was built in a chequer pattern of flint and stone. Attached to it is a short, three-bay nave with a superb, 15th-century roof. This has figures of saints and angels supporting the cross beams and heraldic bosses. The interior is flooded with light and there are also a couple of fragments of medieval stained glass.

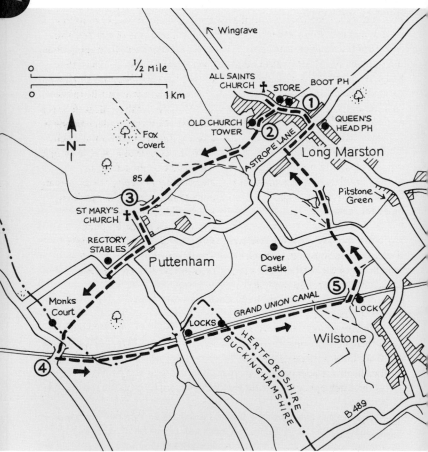

Walk 47 Directions

① From the crossroads by the **Queen's Head** pub walk north along **Station Road** which curves past the **Boot** pub. Continue past the war memorial to visit the Victorian Church of All Saints. Return to the war memorial. Now turn right, down **Chapel Lane**, towards the medieval tower of the old church, set amid trees beyond the thatched **Old Church Cottage**.

Walk 47

② Opposite, go through a five-bar gate and walk diagonally across the field to a stile. Cross a track and climb another stile to walk along the right-hand side of a stream and hedge through two large fields. At the end follow the hedge on the right to a gate. Cross a footbridge and stile then head for a footbridge in the far left corner of the next field, ignoring the stile away to the right. Over the footbridge, turn right to another one and, once over this, walk across pasture to **Puttenham church**.

③ Follow the lane, past the **Cecilia Hall**, to a road junction. Turn right to walk along the road, but, where it turns left, carry straight on, past **Rectory Stables**. At some modern farm cottages go left over a stile by a footpath sign to follow the hedge south then west, around two sides of a field. Over a stile and through another field, the next hedge and stile is the Buckinghamshire county boundary. Crossing a track, the path passes alongside some corrugated iron sheds. When you reach a track, head for the canal bridge beyond its 10-ton limit signs.

④ Walk over **bridge No 8**, then descend to the canal tow path; follow this through **bridge No 7**, past two locks, to **bridge No 5**.

⑤ Leave the tow path and cross bridge No 5. Bear right to follow the left-hand side of a hedge and stream. Over a stile by a gate, follow the path through two fields, then cross a lane and head north along a green lane, ignoring a stile to the left. Shortly, climb a stile to follow a somewhat overgrown lane beside a stream. Emerging from the scrub, cross the corner of a field, leaving it over a stile to the left of an electricity pole. The path crosses an arable field to a footbridge. Two more stiles bring you to a lane (**Astrope Lane**) and a public footpath sign, 'Wilstone 1 mile'. Turn right to walk back to the crossroads in **Long Marston**.

Aldbury's Transport Arteries

A walk from the picture-postcard village of Aldbury, across the railway, along the Grand Union Canal and up to the woods of Aldbury Nowers.

•DISTANCE•	5 miles (8km)
•MINIMUM TIME•	2hrs
•ASCENT / GRADIENT•	230ft (70m) ▲▲▲
•LEVEL OF DIFFICULTY•	🚶 🚶 🚶
•PATHS•	Bridleways, field paths, canal tow path, woods, 1 stile
•LANDSCAPE•	Chalk hills, golf course, fields and a canal
•SUGGESTED MAP•	aqua3 OS Explorer 181 Chiltern Hills North
•START / FINISH•	Grid reference: SP 965124
•DOG FRIENDLINESS•	Beware of horses near Park Hill Farm, and, later, airborne golf balls
•PARKING•	Around green in centre of Aldbury or in public car park up Stocks Lane at north end of village
•PUBLIC TOILETS•	None on route

BACKGROUND TO THE WALK

Aldbury is one of Hertfordshire's most attractive and best-known villages. It nestles in the lee of a steep, wooded chalk escarpment, the stone column of the Bridgewater Monument crowning the ridge to its north east. To the north west the wooded Aldbury Nowers terminate the chalk escarpment from Ivinghoe before dropping nearly 300ft (91m) into the valley of the River Bulbourne. Part of the Chiltern Hills, these ridges frame a dry valley that runs northwards – the southern end gives Aldbury its superb setting. The triangular village green is complete with a pond and old stocks. Huddled around it are fine cottages and houses, including the timber-framed and partly medieval Old Manor House, a photographer's favourite. Stocks Lane runs north from the green. Here you'll see some 17th-century, timber-framed houses, and others of brick, mostly 18th- and 19th-century farm labourers' cottages.

In the 19th century Lord Brownlow of Ashridge, the Lord of the Manor, improved the estate and built cottages in the village, identified by his initial 'B' and the date on a plaque. His developments included the communal bakery (near the church), which has a distinctive chimney. The parish church contains some well-preserved monuments. In the field to its north are what may be the earthworks of a long-demolished manor house.

The Railway Cutting

Heading westwards, our route crosses the railway line that cuts through the Chilterns via the Berkhamsted Gap. This was built as the London-to-Birmingham railway from Euston. The line runs in a cutting that is over 2 miles (3.2km) long and up to 57ft (17m) deep – a major feat of engineering. The line opened as far as Tring Station in October 1837, then to Birmingham the following year. A railway hamlet grew up here, the railway labourers' cottages being numbered in sequence from Euston, so these were Nos 274 to 284 (subsequently renumbered Nos 7 to 17). Beside the railway station the company built a hotel and posting house. The Royal Hotel of 1838 has a grand front block, being three storeys of stucco with a portico. To its rear was a long range of stables, coach-houses and staff accommodation. All this has since been converted to flats and apartments (although still marked 'Hotel' on the map).

Canals Cut Costs

Later in the walk, but 40 years back in time, is the canal. As the railway was to do later, it utilised the Bulbourne Valley. The canal was built by the Grand Junction Canal Company, formed in 1793. (Renaming to the Grand Union Canal occurred in 1929.) The company's canal significantly shortened the route to London from Birmingham by avoiding the winding Oxford Canal and the River Thames. The canal reached Kings Langley in September 1797. As the Chilterns proved difficult to pass, it needed a major cutting – some 30ft (10m) deep – to reduce the number of locks required. It was finally opened in May 1800 and our route follows a good, deep section of the Tring Cutting.

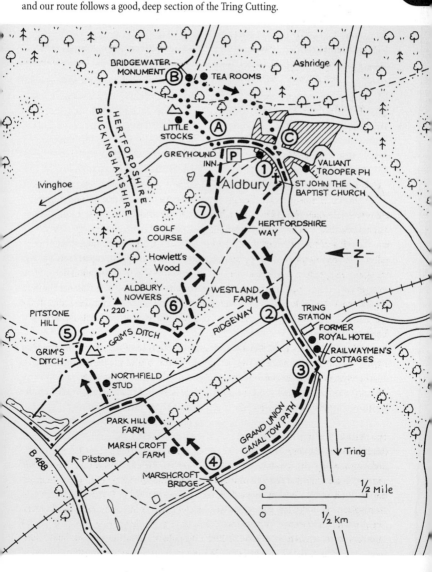

Walk 48

Walk 48 Directions

① From the village green, visit **St John the Baptist Church**. Leave via the lychgate. Turn right to a kissing gate, signposted 'Pitstone Hill', and turn right on to the **Hertfordshire Way**. Past some farm buildings and across a track, the path climbs gently between a hedge and a fence. At the crest turn left on to a bridleway, with a golf course on your right. Descend to join the **Ridgeway National Trail**, which reaches the road via the drive to **Westland Farm**.

② Follow the road, cross the **Northfield Road** junction and then the railway in its cutting. Passing **Tring Station** and the former Royal Hotel and cottages, on the right of the bridge descend steps to the **Grand Union Canal** tow path.

> **WHERE TO EAT AND DRINK**
> There are refreshments around the green in Aldbury. The **Greyhound Inn** has been a pub since 1760. Opposite are the **Town Farm Tea Rooms**. Another pub, the **Valiant Trooper**, is south of the green, down Trooper Road.

③ This canal bridge is Number 135. Follow the tow path beside the canal in its cutting as far as the next bridge, the un-numbered **Marshcroft Bridge**, where you climb up to the lane.

④ Turn right on to the lane to **Marsh Croft Farm**. Go across the railway and through a gate on to a concrete road. Pass **Park Hill Farm**, then some horse paddocks. At the road turn left and pass the gates to **Northfield Stud** and a copse. Turn right beyond, to a footpath sign set back from the road, 'Pitstone and

> **WHAT TO LOOK FOR**
> At Point ⑤ you turn right to join **Grim's Ditch**. Look to your left for a view of this great linear boundary ditch, dating from the Iron Age, and embankment. It continues north across the downland of Pitstone Hill. Grim (or Odin) was an Anglo-Saxon god – these mysterious works are clearly his handiwork!

Pitstone Hill'. Go through the gate on to the path skirting some old chalk pits. Go across a footpath junction to climb steeply alongside woodland, with downland on the left, to reach **Pitstone Hill**.

⑤ Turn right through a kissing gate into the woods of **Aldbury Nowers**. Here the path follows a section of **Grim's Ditch** along the ridge until, descending, you veer left down some steps. At a footpath junction, where the **Ridgeway** turns right, go left. At a guidepost go straight on, initially in the woods, ignoring a path to the right.

⑥ Go through a kissing gate and across a track. The path, now on a golf course, curves downhill through young trees, then turns left at the hedge. At a sign go right and keep on the metalled track, with a hedge right. At the next hedge go through a kissing gate, the path now between high hedges.

⑦ Turn left on to a bridleway to the road (Point Ⓐ on Walk 49). Turn right to follow **Stocks Lane** back to **Aldbury** village.

> **WHILE YOU'RE THERE**
> **Pitstone Windmill** stands isolated in a huge corn field near Ivinghoe village, about 2½ miles (4km) north west of Aldbury. It was fully restored in the 1960s and is open to the public on some summer Sundays.

The Bridgewater Monument

Climb to the Doric column commemorating the Duke of Bridgewater, the 'Father of Inland Navigation'.
See map and information panel for Walk 48

•DISTANCE•	6¼ miles (10.1km)
•MINIMUM TIME•	3hrs
•ASCENT / GRADIENT•	280ft (85m) ▲▲ ▲▲ ▲
•LEVEL OF DIFFICULTY•	👥 👥 👥

Walk 49 Directions (Walk 48 option)

Extend Walk 48 by turning left up the lane at Point Ⓐ. Shortly, at the top of the bank, turn right over a stile and alongside a hedge, towards the wooded slopes. Halfway up, go left through the hedge over a stile. Head diagonally right, uphill, across cattle pasture to a stile on the edge of the wood, well to the right of **Little Stocks**.

Over the stile the path climbs steeply through the woods marked by waymarker posts or arrows painted on trees. Near a cottage veer right, then left with open downland to the right, now climbing gently. When you meet a track go left, back into the woods. At a metalled track turn right, to the **Bridgewater Monument**, Point Ⓑ.

The monument was erected in 1832 to commemorate Francis Egerton, Duke of Bridgewater. He was a canal-building pioneer, his 1755 Bridgewater Canal in Lancashire was the first of the 18th-century canal boom. The inscription on the monument refers to him as 'The Father of Inland Navigation'. The monument looks down on the Grand Union Canal with which, ironically, he had no connection. It's giant Doric column topped by an urn has a viewing platform at the top. You can normally climb up to this between April and October from noon to 5PM at weekends and on Bank Holidays.

Looking to the east you will see the battlemented Bridgewater mansion of **Ashridge** 1½ miles (2.4km) away (► Walk 43). Beyond the monument are the National Trust's tea rooms and a visitor centre and toilets. Sometimes there is also a welcome ice cream van parked near by.

Leave the green past the tea rooms and **Monument Cottage** on a public bridleway, waymarked 'Ashridge Estate Boundary Trail'. Descending on the metalled track, ignoring the 'No Horses' left turn and keeping on the trail, which here is, briefly, also the **Hertfordshire Way**. At a fork bear right to continue on the Hertfordshire Way (the Ashridge Boundary Trail bears left). The descent steepens into a holloway track, leading to the road in **Aldbury**. Turn right to the **village green** – Point Ⓒ and the end of both Walks 48 and 49.

Walk 50

The Canal Reservoirs

Birdlife abounds on the reservoirs of Marsworth and Wilstone.

•DISTANCE•	4½ miles (7.2km)
•MINIMUM TIME•	2hrs
•ASCENT / GRADIENT•	70ft (21m)
•LEVEL OF DIFFICULTY•	
•PATHS•	Tow paths, tracks, some fields, 12 stiles
•LANDSCAPE•	Gentle clayland of Vale of Aylesbury and four great canal reservoirs, now nature reserves
•SUGGESTED MAP•	aqua3 OS Explorer 181 Chiltern Hills North
•START / FINISH•	Grid reference: SP 919140
•DOG FRIENDLINESS•	Lots of birds on reservoirs (plus plenty of other dogs)
•PARKING•	Startops End Reservoir car park, Marsworth, B489
•PUBLIC TOILETS•	None on route

Walk 50 Directions

From the **Startops Reservoir car park** go to the **Grand Union Canal**, to the left of the **Bluebells Tea Room**. Turn left on to the tow path and walk under Bridge 132. At the canal junction go left, signed 'Aylesbury 6¼ miles', on to the Aylesbury Arm. This part of the canal was completed in 1814 and is remarkable for its narrow – 7ft (2.1m), locks. Keep on the tow path, passing six locks, until Bridge 2, known locally as **Dixon's Gap Bridge**. Through the bridge go left over a stile to a footpath alongside a hedge, then along an overgrown green lane into **Wilstone** village.

Wilstone is notorious for Hertfordshire's last witch hunt. A so-called witch, Ruth Osbourn, was murdered here in 1751. After the inquest, held in the Half Moon pub, Thomas Colley, a local chimney-sweep, was hanged at Hertford. Later his body was hung in chains, at nearby Gubblecote.

In Wilstone check out the **Half Moon** pub and **St Cross Church**. Pass the war memorial and continue down the main street. Beyond **Chapel End Lane** and just before the bend go right, through an iron kissing gate and over a stream. Shortly cross a gravel drive, then another footbridge and head diagonally across pasture to a stile. Cross the road, turn left and follow the path alongside the foot of the reservoir embankment. By the **Wilstone car park** climb steps to the embankment. Turn right, so that the reservoir is to your left.

These reservoirs are now nature reserves and are havens for waterfowl and other birds. You can expect to see tufted ducks, pochard, golden eye, goosander, terns,

---

WHILE YOU'RE THERE

A mile (1.6km) south east along the canal are the **Bulbourne Workshops**, now a British Waterways depot. These are a collection of restored brick and slate workshops and stores, mostly from around 1848.

warblers, buntings, water rail, bitterns, cormorantss, great crested grebes and many others. At various points there are bird hides for you to watch this profusion.

WHAT TO LOOK FOR ⓘ

In the evening around Startops and Marsworth Reservoirs you might be lucky enough to see several **Brandts bats** sweeping through the sky. These rare bats were first recorded here in 1975, their first sighting in Hertfordshire. More likely you will see the commoner Noctule and Daubenton bats hunting insects in the twilight.

Crossing the bridge at the end of the embankment, the path moves into the tree belt along the west side of the reservoir. Keep straight on across a stream, and climb a stile to cross pasture. This leads to another stile and a footbridge at the head of a reedy inlet. Now in an arable field, the path leaves the reservoir and follows a hedge. It turns left and right to skirt two sides of a field. Ahead is the embankment of the **Wendover Arm branch canal**. Halfway towards it go left by a footpath post, then right to climb to the canal tow path. Over a stile turn left along the tow path – here the canal is dry and its bed is filled with scrub. The **Wendover Arm**, opened in 1797, never held water literally or financially – it leaked like a sieve. A stop lock was finally built at Little Tring in 1904 and this stretch became dry. Follow the tow path as it winds along the 400ft (122m) contour until it curves sharply right. Here climb a stile, go left to a gate, then turn right on to a lane.

Just before some cottages turn left, signposted 'Tringford Pumping Station', along a track. Go left at a signpost (on the right is the

pumping station). Over a stile head to a path beneath large horse chestnut trees, to skirt the west side of **Tringford Reservoir**.

Among the many engineering challenges, canal-builders must ensure that enough water is available to replenish their locks many times a day. The Tring Summit of the Grand Junction Canal had many locks up from the south and down into the clay vales to the north, all thirsty for water. The answer was to build reservoirs to store water from local streams and wells, then pump it to the canal as needed. The first was dug in 1802 and is now part of the Wilstone Reservoir. Next came the Marsworth Reservoir in 1806, Tringford in 1816 and Startops End in 1817.

Emerging from the trees and scrub, walk along the reservoir embankment to a road. Turn right and at the start of a lay-by car park, cross the road to go sharp left through a kissing gate. This track curves right and emerges from woodland on to the dam between **Marsworth Reservoir** on your right and **Startops End Reservoir** to your left. At the canal turn left along the tow path. Where the canal bears right go straight on through a gate into **Startops End car park**.

WHERE TO EAT AND DRINK ⓘ

At the beginning of the walk at Startops End are two options. The **Bluebells Tea Room** serves food beyond tea and cakes (accessible from the car park or from the canal tow path south of the bridge). The **White Lion** (north of the road and opposite the car park entrance) is a typical canalside pub, serving food. In Wilstone village there is the **Half Moon** pub and a post office and **general store**.

Walking in Safety

All these walks are suitable for any reasonably fit person, but less experienced walkers should try the easier walks first. Route finding is usually straightforward, but you will find that an Ordnance Survey map is a useful addition to the route maps and descriptions.

Risks

Although each walk here has been researched with a view to minimising the risks to the walkers who follow its route, no walk in the countryside can be considered to be completely free from risk. Walking in the outdoors will always require a degree of common sense and judgement to ensure that it is as safe as possible.

- Be particularly careful on cliff paths and in upland terrain, where the consequences of a slip can be very serious.

- Remember to check tidal conditions before walking on the seashore.

- Some sections of route are by, or cross, busy roads. Take care and remember traffic is a danger even on minor country lanes.

- Be careful around farmyard machinery and livestock, especially if you have children with you.

- Be aware of the consequences of changes in the weather and check the forecast before you set out. Carry spare clothing and a torch if you are walking in the winter months. Remember the weather can change very quickly at any time of the year, and in moorland and heathland areas, mist and fog can make route finding much harder. Don't set out in these conditions unless you are confident of your navigation skills in poor visibility. In summer remember to take account of the heat and sun; wear a hat and carry spare water.

- On walks away from centres of population you should carry a whistle and survival bag. If you do have an accident requiring the emergency services, make a note of your position as accurately as possible and dial 999.

Acknowledgements

Martin Andrew would like to thank all those agencies, landholders and individuals who do so much professional and voluntary work to maintain Hertfordshire's network of footpaths and bridleways.

AA Publishing and Outcrop Publishing Services would like to thank Chartech for supplying aqua3 maps for this book. For more information visit their website: www.aqua3.com.

Series management: Outcrop Publishing Services Ltd, Cumbria
Series editor: Chris Bagshaw
Front cover: Spectrum Colour Library